The Celebrity Illusion

Why the Democratic Party Lost the 2024 Presidential Race

Douglas B Sims, PhD

The Celebrity Illusion

Douglas B Sims, PhD

For more information, or to book an event, contact:
dsims@simsassociates.net

Book design by DB Sims
Cover picture purchased from iStock (*franckreporter*)

ISBN – Paperback: 978-1-966739-20-3
ISBN – eBook: 978-1-966739-10-4

First Edition: May 2025

Please leave a review on Amazon, Goodreads, or any site that you purchased this book as a review is part of the overall experience.

The Celebrity Illusion

Table of Contents

The Celebrity Illusion

Acknowledgements

This book would not have been possible without the unwavering support and encouragement of so many people in my life.

First and foremost, I want to thank my family. Your patience, understanding, and belief in me kept me grounded throughout the long hours of research and writing. Your love has been my anchor, and your support gave me the strength and resolve to see this project through to the end.

To my friends, thank you for always being there. Your wisdom, humor, and timely reminders to step away from the keyboard helped me navigate the more challenging moments. Your presence made the journey lighter and the process more enjoyable.

I am especially grateful to my colleagues. Your insights, honest feedback, and professional guidance helped shape the direction of this book. The opportunity to collaborate with such talented individuals has been both humbling and inspiring. Our thought-provoking conversations pushed me to think deeper, challenge assumptions, and broaden my perspective.

This book also owes much to the vast body of work produced by journalists, researchers, and writers. Your commitment to uncovering truth, sharing knowledge, and contributing to public discourse provided the essential foundation for much of what's explored in these pages. I am indebted to your tireless efforts.

To all who contributed, whether directly or indirectly, please accept my deepest gratitude. This book carries my voice, but it is built on the strength of your support. In many ways, it belongs to all of us.

Foreword

The Mirage of Stardom in American Politics

America didn't just lose its way in 2024, it lost its reflection. What stared back at voters wasn't a party grounded in policy, purpose, or people. It was a party high on hashtags, drunk on celebrity endorsements, and blinded by its own curated image.

For years, the Democratic Party has aligned itself with Hollywood, Silicon Valley, and the cultural vanguard, building a formidable brand of progressivism that fused politics with pop culture. It worked, until it didn't. In the 2024 election, the Democrats fielded a candidate supported by the full force of celebrity firepower, armed with viral videos, polished speeches, and a platform drenched in symbolism. They dominated airwaves, dazzled social media, and drew the admiration of elite circles.

But on Election Night, none of it mattered.

The votes didn't come. The working-class coalition that once defined Democratic victories stayed home, or worse, voted red. Middle America turned its back on the spectacle. And in a stunning reversal, the party that believed it could win through cultural momentum alone was handed a cold, undeniable defeat.

This book is not a partisan hit job. It's a political autopsy.

The Celebrity Illusion pulls back the velvet curtain to reveal how the Democratic Party mistook visibility for viability, performance for progress, and applause for policy. It examines how a campaign built on curated charisma failed to connect with voters facing skyrocketing rent, crumbling schools, high grocery bills, and job insecurity. It's about the growing disconnect between the party of "the people" and the people who can no longer afford to believe in it.

This story is personal. I've spent my life navigating the worlds of science, education, and government. I've sat in meetings where policy wasn't abstract, it was the deciding factor in whether a young mother got clean drinking water, whether a student could afford to stay in school, or whether an environmental project got the green light. I've watched working families make impossible choices between medication and rent while celebrities gave political speeches from $20 million estates. And I've seen students, brilliant, ambitious, and terrified, choose groceries over textbooks.

So, when I saw the 2024 Democratic campaign unfold like a Hollywood script, I knew something was terribly wrong.

This book traces how the Democratic Party, once the champion of lunch-pail voters and working families, morphed into a machine that elevated symbolism over substance. It tracks the rise of celebrity influencers turned political surrogates, well-intentioned but often tone-deaf, and reveals how an overreliance on cultural capital alienated the very voters Democrats once fought to represent.

But this isn't just a Democratic problem. It's an American one. Both parties have succumbed to the theater of politics, swapping policy debates for branding strategies and turning town halls into televised performances. The difference in 2024 was that one side embraced chaos, and the other, celebrity. And both left average Americans asking, who's fighting for me?

In the pages ahead, we'll dissect the critical moments, missteps, and messaging failures that led to the 2024 defeat. We'll explore how identity politics, media echo chambers, and overconfidence created a political mirage—an illusion so powerful that party leaders believed it reflected reality. We'll also look forward, asking what it will take to rebuild trust, reclaim authenticity, and restore the focus on what truly matters.

This is the story of a party seduced by its own spotlight. It's a warning for any political movement that tries to win hearts without hearing voices. And it's a challenge to every voter, leader, and citizen who still believes democracy should be led—not liked.

The curtain has fallen. Let's examine what was behind it.

Chapter 1

A History of Success

Over the last two decades, the Democratic Party has achieved significant electoral victories, milestones in modern American politics. These wins were not merely the result of traditional campaigning, but were deeply tied to the party's ability to harness cultural influence, celebrity endorsements, and favorable media narratives. From Barack Obama's groundbreaking 2008 campaign to Joe Biden's coalition-driven win in 2020, Democrats demonstrated a keen ability to unite diverse voter bases through social media and tap into the cultural zeitgeist.

Yet while this strategy proved highly effective in the short term, it also exposed long-term vulnerabilities. The momentum generated by celebrity appeal and media support often masked a growing disconnect with large segments of the American electorate. When I first started as an environmental consultant, I saw firsthand how federal policy decisions could greenlight, or stall, projects overnight. Politics wasn't abstract; it shaped whether a team like mine had work or waited. That experience gave me a front-row seat to how political decisions, far removed from campaign speeches and Hollywood endorsements, directly impacted jobs, communities, and the environment.

This disconnect has only deepened as the Democratic Party increasingly leaned into celebrity culture and symbolic appeals. While effective in energizing parts of the base, this approach has come at a cost: the alienation of working-class and rural voters who once formed the backbone of the party, and who now see it as more concerned with spectacle than substance.

Celebrity endorsements became a hallmark of modern Democratic campaigns. Public figures such as Oprah Winfrey, Beyoncé, and George Clooney didn't just lend their names, they actively campaigned for candidates, using their platforms to mobilize voters and amplify Democratic messaging. Oprah's endorsement of Barack Obama during the 2008 primaries, for instance, was credited with swaying millions of votes and helping elevate his candidacy into a national movement (Garthwaite & Moore, 2013). These endorsements were often aimed at younger and more diverse demographics, creating the perception of cultural momentum that translated into record-breaking voter turnout (Teen Vogue, 2024).

The integration of celebrity culture including former presidents into political campaigns expanded further in subsequent elections. During the 2020 presidential race, former Presidents like Barack Obama, Bill Clinton, and even pseudo celebrity Michelle Obama, stars like Lady Gaga, LeBron James, and others became highly visible proponents of the Democratic platform. Through social media, they reached millions of followers with viral campaigns and calls to action. For example, Taylor Swift's 2024 endorsement of Kamala Harris triggered a 530% spike in voter engagement on Vote.org (Teen Vogue, 2024). While this approach galvanized urban and progressive voters, it also highlighted a growing disconnect with rural and working-class communities. Many of these voters felt alienated by what they perceived as an overemphasis on celebrity-driven politics, which seemed distant from the economic and social issues they faced daily (Henderson, 2021; Harlem View, 2024).

In addition to celebrity culture, the Democratic Party has traditionally benefited from favorable media coverage. Barack Obama's 2008 campaign, in particular, was celebrated by major media outlets as a transformative moment in American history. The framing of Obama's candidacy as a symbol of hope and progress resonated deeply with voters across the country, consolidating support among a broad coalition. However, this reliance on media narratives has its risks. Scholars argue that the favorable portrayal of Democratic candidates and policies can create an echo chamber, where party leaders become insulated from the realities of an increasingly polarized electorate. This dynamic was particularly evident in 2016 and 2024, where overconfidence based on media coverage contributed to underestimating Republican opponents (McDonald, 2020; Patterson, 2013; 2024).

The Obama coalition, forged during his campaigns in 2008 and 2012, represented a new blueprint for Democratic success. This coalition brought together young voters, minorities, women, and highly educated individuals under a unified message of change. Obama's charisma, combined with his ability to articulate a vision that transcended traditional political divides, created an unprecedented level of enthusiasm. Minority groups, particularly African Americans, turned out in record numbers, while younger voters were drawn to his progressive stance on key issues. However, the coalition's strength was deeply tied to Obama himself, and replicating this success proved to be a challenge for subsequent Democratic candidates (Hilton, 2024; López, 2024; Otterbein & Schneider, 2024).

Following Obama's presidency, Joe Biden's 2020 campaign sought to revive this coalition amid the backdrop of a divisive Trump administration. Biden positioned himself as a unifying figure, leveraging endorsements from high-profile figures like Barack Obama and Kamala Harris to rebuild enthusiasm among the Democratic base. His campaign also relied heavily on celebrity support, with performances, endorsements, and viral social media campaigns creating the perception of widespread momentum. Biden's victory demonstrated the enduring potential of the Obama coalition, but it also revealed its fragility. Anti-Trump sentiment played a significant role in uniting disparate voter groups, masking underlying divisions within the Democratic base (Henderson, 2021).

Once in office, Joe Biden faced a complex set of challenges that tested the resilience of the coalition that had propelled him to victory. The high hopes and broad-based support that marked his 2020 campaign quickly began to waver in the face of real-world issues that demanded immediate and effective solutions. Rising inflation emerged as a central concern, eroding the purchasing power of ordinary Americans and fueling discontent among suburban and rural voters who had supported Biden in hopes of economic stability. The lingering effects of the COVID-19 pandemic, coupled with uneven vaccine rollouts and public frustration over shifting health mandates, further exacerbated the administration's challenges. Legislative gridlock, particularly around key priorities like climate change, healthcare reform, and voting rights, highlighted divisions within the Democratic Party and stymied efforts to deliver on campaign promises.

Suburban and rural voters, who had been critical of Biden's narrow victories in swing states, began to feel increasingly neglected. Policies that appeared to favor urban and progressive constituencies, such as aggressive climate initiatives and funding priorities tied to progressive social issues, alienated these key demographics. Many of these voters perceived the administration as more focused on addressing cultural issues and appeasing activist groups than on tackling the bread-and-butter concerns of middle America. While urban centers and progressive strongholds largely remained supportive, the growing discontent in suburban and rural areas presented a significant threat to the Democratic coalition's stability (McDonald, 2020).

At the same time, the Democratic Party continued to rely on celebrity endorsements and favorable media narratives to bolster its image. High-profile figures frequently appeared at events and on social media platforms to praise Biden's administration and its initiatives. However, these endorsements often felt disconnected from the realities faced by working class voters, particularly in regions struggling with economic insecurity and declining industries. While celebrity-driven campaigns succeeded in generating short-term enthusiasm among younger and more culturally liberal voters, they did little to address the frustrations of disaffected groups. This disconnect created an image problem for the Democratic Party, with critics accusing it of being disconnected from reality with the concerns of everyday Americans (Harlem View, 2024).

The Democratic Party's heavy reliance on cultural and symbolic appeals proved effective in rallying enthusiasm during campaigns but revealed significant long-term vulnerabilities in governance. By 2024, the electorate had grown increasingly skeptical of the party's ability to deliver substantive policy changes. Analysts argue that the over-reliance on celebrity endorsements and favorable media coverage fostered a dangerous sense of complacency among Democratic leaders. This complacency, in turn, led to strategic blind spots, such as failing to adequately address the needs of rural voters, overestimating the appeal of progressive policies, and underestimating the growing influence of populist rhetoric from the Republican opposition (Patterson, 2013; 2024; Hilton, 2024; López, 2024; Otterbein & Schneider, 2024).

The history of the Democratic Party's recent successes is a testament to its ability to adapt and innovate in the face of changing political dynamics. Barack Obama's coalition demonstrated the power of unity and hope in mobilizing a diverse electorate, while Joe Biden's presidency showcased the potential for revival in the wake of divisive national leadership. These successes underscore the party's talent for leveraging cultural influence, celebrity endorsements, and media support to achieve electoral victories. However, they also reveal the critical limitations of these strategies when not coupled with substantive engagement with grassroots voters and solutions that address their everyday concerns.

The lessons of the past two decades offer both a roadmap and a warning for the future of Democratic politics. The Obama coalition and Biden presidency highlight the importance of building broad-based support, but sustaining momentum requires more than cultural appeal or symbolic victories. To remain competitive in an increasingly polarized political landscape, the Democratic Party must prioritize policies that resonate across a diverse electorate, engage meaningfully with disaffected groups, and balance cultural influence with tangible governance. The stakes are high, and the path forward demands both introspection and action to ensure the party's relevance and effectiveness in future elections.

Chapter 2

The 2024 Field Takes Shape

The 2024 presidential race began as a tumultuous crossroads in American politics, with the Democratic Party making an unprecedented decision to replace President Joe Biden with Vice President Kamala Harris as their nominee. This move was a gamble—one that showcased the party's willingness to adapt under pressure but also exposed deep vulnerabilities. As Biden's age and health became focal points of Republican criticism, and his approval ratings dipped among key voter demographics, Democratic leaders chose to sidestep the traditional primary process. They placed their hopes on Harris, a historic candidate poised to energize the base with her trailblazing identity as the first Black woman and Asian American nominee. Yet, this bold pivot came with undeniable risks: alienating grassroots supporters, intensifying Republican attacks, and testing the unity of a party already stretched thin by ideological divisions. Meanwhile, the Republican field saw its own upheaval, with a rising star reshaping the GOP's trajectory and setting the stage for a high-stakes showdown that could redefine the nation's political future.

Decision to Replace Biden with Harris

The decision to replace President Joe Biden with Vice President Kamala Harris as the Democratic nominee in the 2024 presidential race marked a pivotal moment in the campaign and had profound political ramifications. This unprecedented move, Harris became the first presidential candidate in modern history to be appointed as the Democratic nominee without participating in a primary process. It reflected both the urgency of the party's concerns and the risks of ignoring voter input. The decision, made amidst growing doubts about Biden's age and perceived vulnerabilities, was framed as a necessary step to maintain the party's competitiveness but introduced significant challenges in terms of unity and public perception.

Biden, at 81, stood at the crossroads of legacy and decline, as mounting scrutiny over his physical vitality and mental sharpness dominated headlines and dinner table debates alike. In an unforgiving political climate, Republican attack ads unleashed a barrage of damning imagery—verbal gaffes looped endlessly, footage of vacant stares slowed for dramatic effect, and moments of hesitation weaponized into a narrative of decline. The message was clear and unrelenting: America, they argued, could no longer afford a commander-in-chief who seemed to shuffle through history rather than lead it (McDonald, 2023). To many critics, he wasn't just running for re-election, he was running against time, gravity, and his own teleprompter.

Behind closed doors, Democratic leadership grappled with declining approval ratings and wavering support among key independent voters, ultimately concluding that Biden's re-election campaign posed too great a risk. Kamala Harris emerged as the alternative—a younger, more dynamic figure who embodied the party's commitment to diversity and progress. Her nomination as the first Black woman and Asian American presidential candidate by a major party was heralded by many as a historic moment. Party strategists believed Harris's candidacy would reinvigorate enthusiasm among key constituencies, particularly Black voters and women, whose turnout had declined since

Barack Obama's elections (Hilton, 2024; López, 2024; Otterbein & Schneider, 2024).

However, Harris's nomination was not without significant controversy and challenges. The decision to forgo the primary process and appoint Harris as the nominee raised concerns about the democratic nature of the selection. Many Democratic voters, particularly those in swing states, expressed frustration at being excluded from the decision-making process, which they felt undermined the party's commitment to voter engagement. The party's top-down decision to bypass the primary process and install Harris as the nominee—an approach aimed at projecting party unity and avoiding intra-party conflict, risked alienating grassroots supporters who viewed the move as elitist, undemocratic, and disconnected from the priorities of everyday voters.

In addition, Harris faced substantial skepticism from suburban and moderate voters, key demographics critical for a general election victory. Her tenure as attorney general in California and her perceived lack of visibility during the Biden administration became focal points of criticism. Polls showed hesitancy among voters who questioned her ability to lead on issues like border security, economic reform, and foreign policy (Henderson, 2024). This narrative was compounded by persistent critiques from Republican opponents, who framed Harris as an untested and risky candidate. The abrupt nature of the transition from Biden to Harris further fueled doubts about the party's stability, offering Republicans a clear opening to challenge the Democratic platform.

The ramifications of this decision extended deeply into the Democratic base. Progressive groups celebrated Harris's nomination as a groundbreaking moment for representation and diversity, while centrist Democrats voiced concerns about her appeal to swing voters in critical battleground states. Many felt that the party's increasing reliance on identity politics, while energizing to urban and younger voters, alienated rural and working-class communities whose economic concerns often went unaddressed (Cramer, 2016; Fiorina et al., 2011).

To be clear, the Republican Party has also leaned on celebrity figures—from Donald Trump himself to media influencers like Tucker Carlson and Joe Rogan. But whereas Republicans often use these personalities to amplify populist sentiment, Democrats have tended to wield celebrity to project cultural sophistication—an approach that has increasingly alienated middle America.

The nomination of a candidate primarily celebrated for her status as a woman of color, rather than for a broadly shared perception of her leadership ability, sparked uncomfortable conversations within the party. It revealed that symbolic milestones, while meaningful, could not substitute for widespread confidence in a candidate's competence and vision. These fractures underscored a broader challenge for the Democratic Party: balancing its progressive values with the need to maintain a broad, inclusive coalition capable of winning elections.

Leading a School of Science, Engineering, and Mathematics with over 20,000 students through record inflation, not once did a celebrity help them pay their rent.

I didn't see anyone from Hollywood show up when students had to choose between textbooks and groceries. This isn't theoretical for me; I've been on the ground, making tough calls, not virtue-signaling on social media. Real leadership isn't about optics; it's about outcomes. It's about showing up, especially when the cameras aren't rolling.

By appointing Kamala Harris as the nominee, the Democratic Party took a bold but contentious step. While her historic candidacy represented progress and a break from the past, it also highlighted the party's internal divisions and vulnerabilities. The decision to bypass the primary process left many questioning the inclusivity and accountability of the Democratic leadership, setting the stage for a contentious and unpredictable general election campaign. Harris's ability to unite the party, win over skeptical voters, and effectively counter Republican attacks would ultimately determine the success of this unprecedented political gamble.

The Rise of an Unexpectedly Formidable Candidate

While the Democratic Party was navigating internal challenges, the Republican Party underwent an unexpected transformation. Early speculation suggested that Donald Trump, still a polarizing figure within the GOP, would dominate the primary field. His strong base of loyal supporters and enduring influence over party leadership positioned him as the presumed frontrunner. However, by mid-2023, the emergence of Donald Trump as a formidable contender reshaped the dynamics of the race and marked a pivotal moment in the Republican Party's evolution.

Trump, a relative newcomer to national politics, as with his first run in the 2016 race, he quickly gained traction with his charismatic leadership, sharp communication skills, and pragmatic approach to issues like the economy, education, and immigration reform. Unlike Trump, whose divisive rhetoric and polarizing policies continued to alienate moderate Republicans and independent voters, once again, Trump presented a fresh and compelling alternative. He appealed to traditional conservatives while successfully reaching suburban women and moderates, demographics critical for a general election victory (Patterson, 2013; 2024).

Trump's meteoric rise in the primaries was fueled by a series of strong debate performances, during which he laid out a clear and actionable vision for America's future. By balancing the populist rhetoric that resonated with the GOP base with thoughtful, policy-oriented solutions, he managed to attract significant media attention and build a coalition that spanned the ideological spectrum of the Republican Party. Trump's ability to distance himself from other candidates most controversial policies while maintaining his appeal to working-class voters marked a significant shift in the Republican narrative, moving toward Trumpism all-encompassing and forward-looking platform (McDonald, 2023).

This shift presented a unique challenge for the Democrats, who were banking on Trump's polarizing candidacy to drive voter turnout. Trump's appeal to suburban voters, women, and working-class communities threatened to undercut key elements of the Democratic coalition. His focus on addressing inflation, creating jobs, downsizing government, and securing the border resonated strongly with voters who had grown increasingly disillusioned with the Biden administration's handling of these issues. By the time Trump secured the Republican nomination, he had positioned himself as a formidable opponent to Kamala Harris, framing his campaign as one of unity, competence, and pragmatism (Henderson, 2024).

In contrast, Kamala Harris's campaign, while preaching unity, often engaged in divisive rhetoric designed to weaponize the political climate against Trump. Kamala's campaign regularly emphasized the dangers of Trump's leadership, even after it became clear that Trump would be the Republican nominee. This strategy aimed to energize the Democratic base by framing the Republican Party as an existential threat to democracy and progress. However, this approach backfired among independents and moderates, who viewed it as out of step with Harris's professed message of national unity. Critics argued that her campaign leaned heavily on identity politics and adversarial messaging rather than addressing the economic and social concerns most pressing to voters (Cramer, 2016; Fiorina et al., 2011).

Harris's campaign also faced scrutiny for its perceived reliance on cultural and symbolic appeals over substantive policy solutions. While her nomination as the first Black woman and Asian American presidential candidate was a historic milestone, it did not shield her from criticisms of her record or her ability to connect with key voter demographics. Her campaign's focus on vilifying Trump often came across as blind to the average American middle-class realities is their race against Trump, a candidate with his own distinct vision and ability to unify the Republican base. This miscalculation left Harris vulnerable to accusations of divisiveness and missed opportunities to articulate a cohesive plan for addressing inflation, healthcare, and border security, issues that dominated voter concerns (Patterson, 2013; 2024).

Trump capitalized on these missteps, positioning himself as a candidate focused on uniting the country and delivering practical solutions. His campaign drew a sharp contrast with Harris's, emphasizing competence, inclusivity, and a departure from the combative tone that had characterized much of the political discourse in recent years. This dynamic set the stage for a highly competitive and deeply consequential general election, where the stark differences in leadership styles and policy priorities between Trump and Harris would dominate the national conversation.

In this unexpected electoral landscape, the Republican Party's transformation under Trump and the Democratic Party's reliance on divisive tactics revealed broader shifts in American politics. The 2024 presidential race became not just a referendum on Trump's legacy but also a test of whether unity and pragmatism could triumph over polarization and identity-driven appeals.

Economy, Inflation, and Key Voter Concerns Shaping the Race

As the 2024 presidential race took shape, the economy emerged as the dominant issue for voters across the political spectrum. Rising inflation, stagnant wage growth, and concerns about the federal government's fiscal policies shaped the political discourse, forcing both parties to craft their platforms around economic recovery.

Inflation had been a persistent issue since the early 2020s, driven by supply chain disruptions, increased government spending, and global economic instability. By 2024, the cost of living had become a central concern for middle-class families, with polling indicating that over 70% of Americans viewed the economy as the most important issue in the election (Reuters, 2024; Scherer, 2024). Both parties faced pressure to present clear solutions, but their approaches diverged significantly.

The Democratic platform, led by Kamala Harris, emphasized continued investment in clean energy, education, and healthcare as pathways to long-term economic stability. However, critics argued that these policies did little to address the immediate financial pressures faced by everyday Americans. Republican nominee Donald Trump, in contrast, focused on reducing inflation by cutting federal spending, lowering taxes, and incentivizing domestic manufacturing. His proposals, while criticized by Democrats as overly simplistic, resonated with voters who were frustrated with rising prices and stagnant wages (McDonald, 2023).

Key voter concerns extended beyond inflation. Suburban and rural voters cited issues like job security, immigration reform, and education as critical to their decision-making. While Harris's campaign leaned heavily on cultural and identity-driven appeals, Trump's focus on tangible policy solutions and economic pragmatism gave him an edge with undecided voters. By the final months of the campaign, it was clear that the economy would be the defining battleground of the 2024 race.

Chapter 3

The Power of the Party Machine

In the high-stakes arena of the 2024 presidential race, the Democratic Party's vaunted political machine, its grassroots mobilization, expansive donor network, and deep ties to Hollywood, faced an unprecedented stress test. For decades, these elements have formed the backbone of Democratic campaigns, securing victories with a blend of cultural influence and organizational prowess. Yet, as the party rallied behind Kamala Harris following Joe Biden's withdrawal, these once-reliable strengths revealed their fragility in a shifting political landscape. The ground game struggled to rekindle enthusiasm among disillusioned voters, the donor network sparked debates over priorities and influence, and Hollywood endorsements, while flashy, deepened cultural divides. The 2024 election showcased the double-edged nature of these resources, as the Democrats grappled with how to channel their historic advantages into a cohesive strategy capable of winning over an increasingly fragmented electorate.

Ground Game, Donors, and Hollywood Connections

The Democratic Party has long been renowned for its sophisticated party machine, which combines grassroots organizing, robust financial backing, and cultural influence on secure electoral victories. In the modern political era, the party's success has often hinged on its ability to mobilize voters, raise substantial funds, and leverage the star power of Hollywood to shape public perception and energize its base. However, while these resources have traditionally been pillars of Democratic strength, the 2024 election revealed both their limits and vulnerabilities.

Ground Game: Mobilizing the Base

The Democratic Party's ground game has long been regarded as one of its most formidable strengths, built on a foundation of grassroots organization, volunteerism, and robust local leadership. Historically, this network has played a pivotal role in mobilizing voters, as demonstrated in landmark campaigns like Barack Obama's 2008 and 2012 elections. During these campaigns, the party combined grassroots efforts with cutting-edge voter data analytics to identify, engage, and mobilize potential supporters. By employing highly personalized outreach strategies, they maximized voter turnout and secured decisive victories (Hilton, 2024; López, 2024; Otterbein & Schneider, 2024).

Fast-forward to the 2024 election, the Democratic ground game retained its ambitious scope but faced significant challenges. Organizers concentrated their efforts in critical battleground states such as Pennsylvania, Michigan, and Arizona, blending modern digital outreach techniques with traditional door-to-door canvassing. Despite this effort, cracks in the system began to surface, revealing a stark contrast to the successes of earlier years. Enthusiasm among key voter groups, including younger voters and working-class communities, appeared to falter. Analysts noted that turnout levels failed to meet expectations, contributing to a sense of unease within the party.

This decline was attributed to several interconnected factors. Economic hardships left many voters disillusioned, while skepticism regarding Kamala Harris's candidacy created additional headwinds. Critics also pointed to a sense of complacency among party leadership, who seemed to assume that past strategies would guarantee present success. Together, these elements undermined the party's ability to fully capitalize on its historically strong ground game, raising concerns about its long-term efficacy and the challenges of maintaining grassroots momentum in a changing political landscape (Henderson, 2024).

The Role of Donors

The Democratic Party's fundraising ($2.05 billion) apparatus has historically been one of its most powerful assets, consistently outpacing its Republican ($1.43 billion) counterparts in securing campaign funds. The party has cultivated a diverse and robust donor base, drawing support from small-dollar grassroots contributors as well as affluent individuals and corporate PACs. This breadth of financial backing has enabled the party to mount extensive and sophisticated campaigns, leveraging contributions from sectors like Silicon Valley, Wall Street, and Hollywood to set fundraising records in 2024 (McDonald, 2023).

The financial composition of political leadership has become a focal point in discussions about party dynamics and voter representation. Critics argue that a significant number of leaders in both major parties are millionaires or billionaires, which may distance them from the everyday experiences of average citizens. As of 2020, over half of the members of the United States Congress were millionaires, with a median net worth of approximately $1 million (Brookings, 2024; PolitiFact, 2024).

This concentration of wealth among political leaders has intensified critiques of the Democratic Party's fundraising strategies. Critics contend that heavy reliance on affluent donors' risk alienating grassroots supporters and compromising the party's commitment to addressing economic disparities (PolitiFact, 2024). Progressive activists have voiced concerns that the influence of wealthy contributors may lead to policy compromises on critical issues such as income inequality and climate change (The New Yorker, 2024). They argue that this dependence on large donors dilutes bold initiatives, leaving the party vulnerable to accusations of prioritizing donor interests over those of everyday Americans.

Furthermore, Republican opponents have leveraged the Democratic Party's associations with affluent elites to portray it as disconnected from the concerns of rural and working-class voters. This narrative, amplified during the 2024 election cycle, complicated the Democrats' efforts to connect with these constituencies (Brookings, 2024). The juxtaposition of the party's financial strength against its challenges in mobilizing certain voter groups underscores the complexities of modern political fundraising and its impact on public perception and electoral outcomes.

Addressing these concerns requires a nuanced approach that balances the necessity of fundraising with the imperative to remain attuned to the diverse economic realities of the electorate. Building trust among grassroots supporters while navigating the influence of affluent donors remains a critical challenge for the Democratic Party as it strives to maintain a broad and inclusive coalition capable of winning elections.

The Two-Party Trap: A Rigged Game

One of the most overlooked, and most corrosive, problems in American politics is not a matter of left versus right. It's the rigged structure of the system itself: the two-party monopoly. For all their fierce performances on cable news and Twitter wars, Republicans and Democrats share one critical, unspoken agreement: preserve the duopoly at all costs.

They'll savage each other in public. But behind the scenes? They are strange bedfellows guarding the same fortress. And nothing threatens them more than the rise of a serious third-party challenger. When one appears, the façade of partisanship crumbles. Together, the two parties, their donors, and their loyal media arms unleash a full-blown assault: mockery, fearmongering, lawsuits, ballot-access roadblocks, debate stage exclusions, and carefully coordinated "spoiler" narratives. It's not about protecting democracy. It's about protecting themselves.

A perfect case study? Ross Perot in 1992.

Running as an independent, Perot tapped into the raw anger of voters fed up with ballooning national debt and a political establishment that seemed more interested in cocktail parties than fiscal responsibility. At one point, he led both George H.W. Bush and Bill Clinton in national polls. Not competitive: leading.

Perot's message was simple: Washington was broken, and both parties were to blame. And that terrified them.

He ultimately captured nearly 19% of the national vote, the best third-party showing since Theodore Roosevelt in 1912. He won no electoral votes, thanks to the rigged, winner-take-all system designed to suffocate third parties. But his influence reshaped the election. Analysts debate whether he hurt Bush more than Clinton, but the truth is simpler: he scared both sides so badly that they worked overtime to make sure no "Perot moment" could happen again.

In the years that followed, both parties quietly fortified the walls:

- Debate commission rules conveniently kept independents off the national stage.

- Ballot access laws in key states were tightened.

- "Spoiler" narratives were pushed harder to shame voters away from third-party candidates.

- Gerrymandering was weaponized to keep seats predictably red or blue.

This wasn't politics. It was cartel behavior.

It still is.

Today, the system isn't built to reflect the diversity of American political thought. It's built to crush it. Voters who dare to look beyond red and blue are told they're "throwing their vote away." Third parties aren't underdogs; they are systematically strangled before they can ever pose a threat.

And why is that so dangerous? Because it robs America of its greatest strength: the ability to adapt, innovate, and evolve. Instead of healthy debate, we get staged outrage. Instead of real choices, we get corporate mascots in red and blue suits. Voters aren't apathetic, they're exhausted by a system rigged to lock out fresh ideas and fresh leadership.

Until Americans rise up and demand real electoral reform, ranked-choice voting, open primaries, fair ballot access, the two-party duopoly will keep choking democracy. It will keep new voices out and entrench the same decaying political elite who talk endlessly about "change" but fear it more than anything.

The two-party system isn't broken.

It's working exactly as designed.

Cultural Capital Meets Political Strategy

The Democratic Party's connection to Hollywood has become a hallmark of its modern brand, reflecting a symbiotic relationship where celebrities bring glamour and attention to the party's causes while advancing their own advocacy goals. However, the Republican Party has increasingly mirrored this strategy, forging ties with conservative-leaning celebrities, influencers, and media personalities to energize its base and shape public narratives, demonstrating that both parties now leverage cultural capital as a political tool in the battle for influence and voter loyalty.

Over the years, high-profile figures have played pivotal roles in fundraising, rallying supporters, and shaping public discourse. In the 2024 election, this relationship remained strong, with stars like Beyoncé, George Clooney, and Jennifer Lawrence leading the charge. They attended rallies, produced high-impact campaign ads, and mobilized millions of followers across social media platforms, merging entertainment with political activism in a way few others could (Hilton, 2024; López, 2024; Otterbein & Schneider, 2024).

Despite its advantages, this strategy revealed significant vulnerabilities. While Hollywood endorsements energized urban centers and progressive strongholds, they often alienated rural and conservative voters, deepening an already growing cultural divide. For many outside the party's base, the prominence of celebrity figures reinforced perceptions that the Democratic Party catered to elites disconnected from the concerns of "everyday Americans." This sentiment was skillfully exploited by the Republican campaign, with candidate Donal Trump framing himself as the voice of "real Americans" against the perceived elitism of the Democrats. His rhetoric painted a vivid contrast between the rural heartland and the Democratic Party's urban, Hollywood-centered identity, resonating with voters who felt overlooked by coastal and cultural elites (Henderson, 2024).

This dynamic underscored the broader challenges of celebrity-driven political strategies. While star power can generate excitement and funds, it risks overshadowing substantive policy discussions and exacerbating divisions between cultural and geographic communities. The 2024 campaign highlighted the double-edged sword of Hollywood's political involvement, forcing Democrats to grapple with how to balance star appeal with broad, inclusive outreach to a diverse electorate.

Celebrity Endorsements as a Double-Edged Sword

What Worked in the Past but Failed in 2024 was celebrity involvement. Celebrity endorsements have long been a cornerstone of the

Democratic Party's election strategy, combining financial clout, widespread visibility, and cultural influence to bolster campaigns. Iconic examples, like Oprah Winfrey's game-changing support for Barack Obama in 2008 and Taylor Swift's voter registration efforts in 2020, illustrate how influential figures can energize key demographics and amplify the party's outreach (Garthwaite & Moore, 2013). These endorsements have been particularly effective in mobilizing younger voters and bridging the gap between pop culture and political engagement.

Yet, the 2024 election highlighted the potential pitfalls of over-reliance on celebrity endorsements. While they continued to inspire enthusiasm in urban centers and progressive circles, their broader appeal was more limited. Critics argued that excessive dependence on high-profile figures alienated rural and working-class voters, reinforcing perceptions of the Democratic Party as disconnected from the realities faced by everyday Americans.

Republican opponents capitalized on this dynamic, portraying Democrats as overly tied to cultural elites and out of step with mainstream concerns. This narrative resonated in key battleground states, where economic challenges and cultural divides overshadowed the allure of celebrity involvement. The 2024 experience underscored the risks of leaning too heavily on star power without addressing the substantive needs of a diverse electorate. As the party moves forward, it must strike a balance between leveraging celebrity influence and crafting inclusive, grounded messages that resonate with voters across all communities.

Successes of Celebrity Endorsements

In past elections, celebrity endorsements have demonstrated remarkable effectiveness in connecting with younger voters and those typically less engaged with traditional political channels. By leveraging their widespread popularity and influence, celebrities have successfully infused political campaigns with a sense of cultural relevance and urgency. For instance, Beyoncé's active involvement in voter registration drives, combined with her high-energy concert performances supporting Democratic candidates, created a compelling narrative that resonated with millennial and Gen Z audiences. Her participation helped frame voting as both a civic duty and a cultural statement, leading to a measurable boost in turnout among younger demographics (Hilton, 2024; López, 2024; Otterbein & Schneider, 2024).

Similarly, Oprah Winfrey's endorsement of Barack Obama during the 2008 Democratic primaries showcased the profound impact a single celebrity can have on an election. Moreover, her advocacy not only brought widespread media attention to Obama's candidacy but also motivated millions of her followers to engage in the political process. Studies estimate that her endorsement alone accounted for over a million votes, demonstrating how celebrity influence can translate directly into electoral gains (Garthwaite & Moore, 2013). These examples highlight the strategic value of celebrity endorsements in mobilizing otherwise disengaged voters, making them a critical tool for modern political campaigns.

The 2024 Backlash

Despite previous successes, celebrity endorsements in the 2024 election turned into a significant liability for the Democratic Party. What once served as a powerful tool for mobilizing voters now appeared superficial, undermining the party's ability to engage in meaningful discussions about critical issues. Critics argued that the Democrats' overreliance on celebrity appeals distracted from pressing concerns such as inflation, job security, and border control. Republican opponents capitalized on this narrative, portraying the Democrats as more invested in Hollywood glamour than addressing the everyday struggles of average Americans (McDonald, 2023).

Kamala Harris's campaign, in particular, came under fire for its heavy use of celebrity surrogates to elevate her visibility. These high-profile endorsements, participate in rallies, and produce campaign ads. While their efforts generated significant media attention, they often failed to resonate with key constituencies, especially working-class and rural voters. For example, Lady Gaga was reportedly paid $2 million for her campaign appearances, and LeBron James received $1.5 million for his involvement in voter mobilization initiatives (Reuters, 2024; Scherer, 2024). However, their messaging often seemed clueless about the issues, focusing on progressive cultural issues rather than the economic hardships many voters were facing.

This strategy backfired spectacularly, with many voters viewing the celebrity-driven campaign as out of touch and insincere. Republican candidates amplified these sentiments, mocking the Democrats for prioritizing endorsements from Hollywood over genuine grassroots engagement. GOP leaders highlighted these high-profile partnerships as evidence of Kamala Harris's inability to connect with everyday Americans, framing her as an elite candidate who relied on star power rather than substantive policy proposals (Reuters, 2024; Scherer, 2024).

The fallout from these endorsements was compounded by high-profile gaffes that embarrassed the Democratic Party. For instance, at a campaign rally in Pennsylvania, a visibly disconnected celebrity advocate referred to a key battleground state as "flyover country," sparking outrage among local voters (Henderson, 2024). These missteps reinforced the perception that the Democratic Party was detached from the needs and values of ordinary Americans, turning what was intended to be a strategic advantage into a source of humiliation. The 2024 election underscored the risks of overreliance on celebrity endorsements, forcing the party to reconsider its approach to voter engagement.

The Changing Role of Celebrity Influence

The 2024 election exposed a broader shift in the effectiveness of celebrity influence in politics, marking a stark departure from its previous successes. While social media platforms enabled celebrities to directly engage millions of followers, the fragmentation of media consumption often meant their messages failed to break through to undecided voters. The hyper-polarization of American politics further compounded the issue. Celebrity endorsements, once perceived as bipartisan expressions of civic duty, were increasingly viewed as overtly partisan acts. Rather than inspiring unity, these endorsements often alienated as many voters as they rallied, undermining their intended impact (Henderson, 2024).

For decades, the Democratic Party's resources, including a robust ground game, a vast donor network, and strong ties to Hollywood, have been cornerstones of its electoral strategy. However, the 2024 election revealed the limitations of these approaches in an era of heightened political division and widespread economic anxiety. Despite these efforts, their involvement often seemed tone-deaf, focusing on cultural and social issues rather than addressing the pressing economic challenges faced by working-class Americans.

The financial investments in these endorsements only heightened the embarrassment for the Democratic Party. These paid celebrities sparked backlash from voters, who saw the expenditures as wasteful and emblematic of a party is detached from the public's with everyday concerns. Adding to the humiliation, several celebrity advocates made high-profile missteps. At a Pennsylvania rally, one celebrity mistakenly referred to the state as "flyover country," a term often resented by local residents. Another incident involved a celebrity comparing the struggles of rural voters to those of Hollywood elites, a remark widely derided as clueless and condescending.

These failures left not only the Democratic Party but also the celebrities themselves with egg on their faces. Many of the high-profile figures faced ridicule on social media and in the press for their perceived ineffectiveness and detachment. Republican opponents seized on these gaffes, amplifying the narrative that the Democratic Party was beholden to out-of-touch elites more concerned with star power than substantive policy solutions. This framing resonated deeply with voters in key battleground states, further eroding the party's credibility among undecided and working-class voters.

The 2024 election served as a sobering reminder of the risks inherent in over-reliance on celebrity endorsements. While they succeeded in energizing parts of the Democratic base, they ultimately underscored the party's disconnect from critical voter groups, reinforcing perceptions of elitism and insincerity. As the Democratic Party looks ahead, it faces the challenge of adapting its strategies to a rapidly changing cultural and political landscape. The era of celebrities as surefire political assets appears to be waning, demanding a reevaluation of how the party connects with an increasingly fragmented and diverse electorate.

Chapter 4

Ignoring the Kitchen Table Issues

The 2024 election highlighted a critical misstep in modern political strategy: the failure to prioritize the "kitchen table issues" that dominate the lives of everyday Americans. While progressive social policies addressing systemic inequities and long-term societal goals hold undeniable value, they often overshadow the immediate concerns of inflation, stagnant wages, and skyrocketing costs of living. For many working- and middle-class voters, the rising cost of groceries, rent, and healthcare presents a far more pressing reality than debates over aspirational reforms. As a college dean overseeing over 20 thousand students each semester, I watched bright young minds choose between buying books and paying rent—while politicians debated hashtags and soundbites. This disconnect between party priorities and voter needs has not only alienated key constituencies but also fostered a growing perception of political leaders as being disconnected from reality with the struggles of ordinary families. In an era where economic anxieties run high, the inability to address these bread-and-butter issues risks reshaping the political landscape and undermining trust in leadership.

The Overemphasis on Progressive Social Policies

Progressive social policies, while central to the platform of modern liberal movements, often overshadow critical "kitchen table issues" such as inflation, wages, and the cost of living. These policies, focusing on addressing systemic injustices and achieving inclusivity through measures like criminal justice reform, expanded healthcare access, and environmental sustainability, align closely with long-term societal goals. However, many middle- and working-class voters report feeling alienated by this focus, particularly when economic struggles dominate their daily lives (Abramowitz, 2023). The dissonance arises when these groups perceive that their immediate needs, affording groceries, paying rent, and securing stable employment, are not receiving the urgent attention they require.

For instance, initiatives surrounding climate justice and equity in education, while undeniably significant, can feel disconnected from the immediate financial pressures facing families. While climate action promises long-term environmental and economic benefits, policies such as carbon taxes or aggressive renewable energy transitions often translate into higher energy costs for households in the short term (Miller & Thompson, 2022). Similarly, while expanding access to higher education is a commendable goal, families struggling with stagnant wages and mounting bills may view tuition reforms as less pressing compared to the rising cost of everyday essentials. For many voters, these policies symbolize a leadership focused on distant, aspirational goals rather than pragmatic, actionable solutions to their present struggles.

The 2022 midterm elections vividly illustrated this dynamic. Candidates who framed their campaigns around economic recovery and cost-of-living improvements, such as reducing inflationary pressures or increasing wage growth, performed better in battleground districts than those who centered their platforms on progressive social agendas (Pew

Research Center, 2023). Voters in economically vulnerable regions expressed frustration with what they perceived as misplaced priorities, signaling that policies addressing inflation, housing affordability, and job creation resonated more than those emphasizing identity politics or environmental reforms. This trend underlined a critical lesson for political leaders: addressing systemic inequities is important, but failing to confront the bread-and-butter economic issues that shape daily life can lead to significant electoral consequences.

Moreover, the emphasis on progressive social policies risks creating a perception of elitism among political leaders. Critics argue that such policies often reflect the priorities of highly educated urban constituencies, which do not always align with the lived experiences of rural or economically disadvantaged voters (Primerica, 2023). This disconnect fosters resentment and exacerbates existing political divides, as middle-class families feel overlooked in favor of policies that they perceive to cater to niche interests or ideological goals. To bridge this gap, leaders must strike a balance between addressing long-term systemic changes and offering immediate economic relief to struggling households. Failure to do so risks alienating a broad swath of voters who are critical to building and sustaining political majorities.

Inflation, Wages, and the Cost-of-Living Crisis

The United States has faced significant economic challenges in recent years, with inflation, stagnant wages, and skyrocketing costs of living becoming major issues for families across the country. These "kitchen table" concerns dominate household conversations, as families struggle to make ends meet amidst rising prices and a widening gap between earnings and expenses. For many, the dream of upward mobility has been replaced by the harsh reality of financial precarity. Despite the severity of these challenges, political leadership has often been criticized for focusing on partisan agendas or long-term reforms, leaving voters feeling neglected and frustrated.

Neither party has shown consistent urgency in addressing the day-to-day financial burdens of working Americans. From rising rent and healthcare costs to stagnant wages and student debt, these issues have long taken a backseat to culture wars, virtue signaling, and donor-class appeasement, regardless of which party holds the White House.

Rising inflation rates have disproportionately impacted lower-income households, exacerbated long-standing economic disparities and creating an environment where financial survival becomes a daily struggle for millions of Americans (Primerica, 2023). For families living paycheck to paycheck, even small increases in the price of basic necessities, such as groceries, housing, and healthcare, can have devastating ripple effects. From 2020 to 2024, the average American household experienced a 13% increase in the cost of essentials (about $1,300 more per month), putting additional strain on already limited budgets and widening the gap between those who can adapt to rising costs and those who cannot (U.S. Bureau of Labor Statistics, 2024).

The economic reality for lower-income families during this period became increasingly dire. Rent hikes outpaced wage growth in many urban and suburban areas, while healthcare costs—already a major burden, rose faster than inflation overall. Many households were forced to make difficult choices between paying for basic needs like medication, utility bills, or transportation. In these communities, the economic challenges fueled by inflation have not only deepened financial hardship but also led to an erosion of trust in political leaders to address these urgent issues effectively.

Despite these mounting pressures, political discourse has often been dominated by debates over social and ideological policies rather than concrete economic solutions. Democrats, in particular, have been criticized for failing to adequately prioritize inflation and cost-of-living concerns in their messaging and policymaking. While acknowledging the importance of tackling systemic inequities and long-term policy challenges, critics argue that leadership has not sufficiently addressed the immediate financial struggles of everyday Americans.

This disconnect is reflected in public opinion. A 2023 Gallup poll revealed that 78% of Americans ranked inflation as their top concern, a figure consistent across demographic and political lines. However, fewer than 30% of respondents believed their representatives were actively working to address the problem, highlighting a significant gap between voter expectations and perceived governmental action (Gallup, 2023). This perception has contributed to growing dissatisfaction with political leadership and has further alienated working-class voters who feel ignored by the Democratic Party's focus on broader progressive goals.

The failure to address inflation in a meaningful way has also had electoral consequences. Swing voters, who play a decisive role in closely contested elections, have increasingly shifted their support toward candidates emphasizing economic recovery and cost-of-living issues. In the absence of visible, tangible progress on these concerns, Democrats risk losing the trust of a critical portion of their base, particularly in economically vulnerable districts where rising costs are most acutely felt.

Addressing inflation and the cost-of-living crisis requires more than acknowledgment—it demands decisive action and clear communication. Voters want to see policies that directly address their everyday struggles, such as measures to control housing costs, stabilize energy prices, and ensure wage growth keeps pace with inflation. Without these efforts, the economic strain on lower- and middle-income families will continue to grow, deepening inequalities and widening the chasm between the electorate and its leaders.

Disconnect Between Party Priorities and Voter Concerns

Numerous polls underscore the disconnect between party agendas and voter preferences, revealing a growing misalignment between what political leaders prioritize and the concerns most important to their constituents. For example, a recent survey conducted by Pew Research found that while Democratic leaders have heavily emphasized social justice reforms, such as equity in education and police accountability, voters overwhelmingly ranked inflation, jobs, and public safety as their top three concerns (Pew Research Center, 2023). This persistent focus on progressive policies, while meaningful to certain segments of the electorate, has left many voters feeling that their immediate economic struggles are being ignored. Such a disconnect has not only widened partisan divides but also fueled a perception that political elites are out of touch with the realities of everyday Americans.

This perception is particularly pronounced among economically vulnerable populations. For working-class voters and those living in rural areas, discussions about progressive reforms often feel disconnected from the practical challenges of putting food on the table, paying bills, or securing reliable transportation. Leaders who champion social policies without addressing these tangible economic concerns risk alienating large swaths of their base. For example, while proposals to reduce college debt and ensure equitable access to healthcare resonate with younger, urban voters, they do little to alleviate the struggles of middle-aged or older voters grappling with rising costs of living and stagnant wages.

Economic concerns also transcend traditional party lines, further complicating the political landscape. An analysis of swing voters in presidential elections revealed that both Democrats and Republicans disproportionately prioritized economic stability over social issues (Larsson, 2021). This finding suggests that voters from across the ideological spectrum are united by a shared frustration over the lack of focus on financial concerns, such as inflation, job creation, and affordable housing. For instance, many swing voters in battleground states expressed disappointment with both parties' inability to propose actionable solutions for addressing inflation and rising healthcare costs, which they viewed as critical to their quality of life.

The data demonstrates that parties must recalibrate their platforms to address economic challenges more effectively. Both Democrats and Republicans have an opportunity to capture the support of disillusioned voters by prioritizing policies that directly address the economic pressures they face. However, this requires a shift in strategy—moving away from divisive rhetoric and ideological posturing toward pragmatic, bipartisan solutions. Policies aimed at reducing inflationary pressures, creating sustainable wage growth, and improving access to affordable housing would resonate across party lines, offering a unifying platform in an increasingly polarized electorate.

Failure to adapt to these priorities' risks alienating key voting blocs and undermining trust in political institutions. As economic pressures continue to mount, voters are increasingly looking for leaders who understand their struggles and are committed to enacting policies that bring tangible improvements to their daily lives. Ignoring these "kitchen table issues" in favor of broader ideological goals will only exacerbate the growing divide between the electorate and its leaders, potentially reshaping the political landscape for years to come.

Chapter 5

The Celebrity Trap

I n an age where celebrity influence permeates every corner of culture and communication, political campaigns have increasingly embraced high-profile endorsements as a tool to energize their base and capture media attention. The allure of a famous face or influential voice can create buzz, draw massive crowds, and generate social media engagement. However, this strategy often comes at a cost. Over-reliance on celebrity endorsements risks alienating key demographics who view such tactics as superficial and is completely detached from Americans realities. For many voters, particularly those in working-class or rural areas, the involvement of wealthy and insulated celebrities can highlight a stark disconnect between political campaigns and the realities of everyday struggles. While celebrities can shine a spotlight on issues, their contributions rarely translate into substantive solutions, and for many, their presence raises questions about the authenticity and priorities of the campaigns they represent (Wood and Herbst, 2007).

This chapter explores how the use of celebrity endorsements has shifted from a complementary campaign tool to a crutch that sometimes overshadows critical policy issues. By examining notable case studies and their fallout, it becomes clear that while celebrities can amplify a message, they can also create unintended divisions and contribute to a growing perception of political elitism.

The Over-Reliance on Star Power and Its Consequences

In an era where social media amplifies celebrity influence and turns endorsements into viral moments, political campaigns have increasingly relied on high-profile figures to promote their platforms and engage with voters. This trend reflects the belief that celebrity involvement can boost visibility, energize younger audiences, and lend campaigns a cultural edge. However, while leveraging star power can draw attention to key issues and elevate campaign narratives, the over-reliance on celebrity endorsements often alienates critical demographics, particularly those who feel disconnected from the world of fame and wealth. For these voters, many of whom face daily struggles related to inflation, healthcare, or job security, the use of celebrities struggles appeared as misreading the room, reinforcing perceptions that political movements prioritize public relations over substantive governance (Wood and Herbst, 2007).

The use of celebrities as political surrogates can often do more harm than good, especially when voters see them as wildly disconnected from reality with real-world struggles. Celebrities live in a bubble—one lined with luxury cars, gated mansions, and private jets, far removed from the financial, social, and emotional hardships that define everyday American life. As of 2019, the median U.S. household income was just $60,030, with a median net worth of $97,300, numbers that wouldn't cover the down payment on a celebrity's vacation home. Meanwhile, many public figures doling out political advice are worth hundreds of millions, if not billions. This obscene wealth gap strips their advocacy of authenticity and breeds deep resentment among voters who feel talked down to by people who have never stood in a food bank line, struggled to pay rent, or worked two jobs to survive.

Policy from the Penthouse: When the Party Forgets Main Street

A new college graduate in Las Vegas earning the average starting salary of $45,000 per year, roughly $3,200 per month after taxes, is finding that the math just doesn't work.

Let's break it down:

- **Rent for a 1-bedroom apartment:** $1,500/month

- **Utilities (electric, water, internet, etc.):** $250/month

- **Student loan payments:** $400/month (conservative estimate)

- **Car payment:** $400/month

- **Car insurance:** $150/month (Nevada has some of the highest rates in the country)

- **Groceries and food:** $400/month

- **Miscellaneous living expenses** (clothing, hygiene, gas, phone, etc.): $400/month

Total monthly expenses: $3,500/month

Monthly take-home pay: $3,200/month

Shortfall: -$300/month

That's without budgeting for emergencies, savings, medical costs, or a social life. In short, a college degree no longer guarantees financial stability—even in a city like Las Vegas, once known for its lower cost of living. Instead, new graduates are often forced to take on roommates, side hustles, or more debt just to cover basic living expenses.

This situation illustrates a painful truth: the cost of adulting has far outpaced entry-level wages. For many young professionals, financial independence isn't delayed by choice, it's delayed by a broken economic system.

Research confirms that Americans drastically overestimate their chances of moving up the economic ladder, an illusion fueled, in part, by elites who sell hope they never had to buy (Kraus & Tan, 2015). Celebrity endorsements, while flashy and headline-grabbing, can backfire spectacularly: studies show they may alienate more voters than they attract, particularly when the messenger appears clueless about the realities they claim to champion (Jackson, 2018). For voters in rural and economically battered communities, the Democrats clueless approach of political stardom doesn't inspire action—it deepens their distrust. It sends a clear message: politics isn't about solving your problems. It's about who can get the most retweets while pretending to understand them.

Why Glitz Doesn't Translate

Moreover, the over-reliance on star power has a polarizing effect on the electorate. While celebrity endorsements can energize existing supporters, they frequently alienate undecided voters or those with opposing viewpoints. This dynamic was evident during the 2022 midterm elections, where high-profile endorsements from Hollywood elites, musicians, and athletes sparked controversy among working-class voters. Many felt their voices were being overshadowed by celebrities whose lifestyles and values seemed far removed from their own. Such perceptions are particularly damaging in battleground regions, where voter priorities are often focused on "kitchen table issues" such as affordable housing, education, and healthcare. In these areas, celebrity involvement can unintentionally deepen political divides, reinforcing the idea that political elites are disconnected from the concerns of ordinary Americans (Miller & Thompson, 2022).

In addition to alienating voters, celebrity endorsements can shift the focus of campaigns away from substantive issues and toward performative gestures. Campaigns that heavily feature star power risk losing control of their messaging, as media coverage and public discourse gravitate toward the personalities involved rather than the policies being promoted. This phenomenon can detract from the campaign's ability to address pressing issues, leaving voters with the impression that the campaign is more about glitz and glamour than governance.

The rise of celebrity influence in politics reflects broader trends in modern media culture, where visibility and social capital often eclipse expertise and authenticity. However, as political campaigns continue to embrace this strategy, they must also contend with its limitations. To resonate with voters across the socioeconomic spectrum, campaigns must prioritize meaningful engagement and policy-driven messaging over the fleeting allure of star power. Only by addressing the real concerns of their constituents can political leaders bridge the growing disconnect between their platforms and the people they aim to serve.

Case Studies of Misaligned Endorsements and Messaging Backfires

The pitfalls of celebrity endorsements are best illustrated through high-profile case studies where campaigns saw unintended consequences from their reliance on star power. These examples highlight the risks of misaligned messaging and the potential backlash when voters perceive insincerity or elitism.

When Celebrity Endorsements Backfire

What was meant to be star power often turns into static. In politics, when celebrity endorsements go wrong, they don't just miss the mark—they magnify the disconnect between the cultural elite and everyday Americans.

Case Study 1: Taylor Swift and the 2018 Midterms

In 2018, pop superstar Taylor Swift broke her political silence to endorse Democratic candidates in Tennessee, marking her first foray into political advocacy. Her announcement, made via Instagram to her millions of followers, was widely lauded by progressives who saw her involvement as a powerful call to action for young voters. However, the endorsement also faced significant backlash from conservative voters in her home state. Critics accused Swift of being disconnected from Tennessee's deeply rooted values and cultural identity, painting her as an outsider imposing her beliefs on local politics. While her post gained massive attention and was credited with increasing voter turnout among younger demographics, it also galvanized conservative opposition. A post-election analysis revealed that, despite the initial enthusiasm, Swift's involvement mobilized conservative groups, contributing to the defeat of Kamala Harris (Wood and Herbst, 2007). This case highlighted the limitations of celebrity influence, especially in regions where local culture and identity play a central role in voter decision-making.

Swift's political engagement resurfaced prominently in the 2024 presidential election, where she publicly endorsed Vice President Kamala Harris. Building on her reputation as a politically conscious celebrity, Swift leveraged her social media platforms to rally support, encouraging young people to register to vote and participate in campaign events. However, the same dynamics that complicated her 2018 involvement were evident once again. While her efforts were praised for energizing a younger, urban audience, they drew criticism from more conservative and working-class demographics who felt alienated by her message. Many perceived her as emblematic of the celebrity elite, far removed from the financial and social struggles faced by everyday Americans.

In battleground states, Swift's endorsement became a polarizing topic, with local voters expressing frustration at what they viewed as an intrusion of Hollywood-style politics into their communities. Conservative commentators framed her involvement as part of a broader Democratic strategy reliant on out-of-touch cultural figures rather than substantive policies. Moreover, her advocacy for progressive social policies, such as LGBTQ+ rights and climate action, resonated strongly with her core audience but alienated voters in rural and conservative-leaning areas who prioritized economic issues like inflation and job security.

Despite the backlash, Swift's endorsement undeniably raised awareness of the Harris campaign and increased engagement among her younger fan base, particularly Gen Z voters. However, as in 2018, the broader impact of her involvement proved to be a double-edged sword. While Swift's advocacy highlighted the potential of celebrities to energize specific voter blocks, it also underscored the risks of relying on star power in regions where cultural identity and economic concerns outweigh celebrity influence. Her involvement in both 2018 and 2024 serves as a cautionary tale about the complexities of celebrity endorsements in American politics, particularly in deeply divided and culturally distinct electorates.

Case Study 2: Oprah Winfrey and Georgia Gubernatorial Race

Oprah Winfrey's involvement in Stacey Abrams' 2018 gubernatorial campaign in Georgia showcased both the power and pitfalls of celebrity endorsements in American politics. Her door-to-door canvassing, impassioned speeches, and national platform brought unprecedented visibility to Abrams' candidacy, significantly boosting turnout among key Democratic demographics—especially African American women. But while Winfrey's support galvanized the Democratic base, it also came with unintended consequences. Some voters saw the campaign as more of a celebrity spectacle than a grassroots effort. In rural and working-class areas, her immense wealth and outsider status clashed with local concerns, reinforcing perceptions that the campaign was disconnected from Georgia's economic and cultural realities (Larsson, 2021).

This pattern reemerged in 2024, when Winfrey endorsed Vice President Kamala Harris in her bid for the presidency. Once again, her influence helped mobilize urban voters and progressive strongholds by spotlighting issues like women's rights, healthcare equity, and racial justice. But as in 2018, critics questioned whether her presence truly helped the candidate reach undecided voters. Many in rural and swing-state communities viewed her high-profile events as elitist distractions that overshadowed pressing concerns like inflation, job security, and housing costs.

One particularly controversial moment came when the Harris campaign paid $2.5 million to Winfrey's production company to host a celebrity-filled town hall. While the event drew media attention and energized liberal audiences, it was widely panned as tone-deaf at a time of rising economic anxiety (New York Post, 2024). For undecided and economically strained voters, the event symbolized what they saw as the campaign's broader weakness: relying too heavily on cultural icons and symbolic messaging instead of offering concrete solutions to everyday struggles (Reuters, 2024).

Ultimately, Winfrey's political activism illustrates a larger dilemma for modern campaigns: while star power can amplify a message, it can just as easily drown it out, especially when voters feel they're being talked at by elites, not heard by equals.

A Pew Research Center survey illustrated just how deep economic anxiety had become, with 74% of Americans expressing serious concern over the price of food and consumer goods, 69% worrying about housing costs, and 40% concerned about job availability—significantly higher than in previous election cycles (Pew Research Center, 2024). In Mesa, Arizona, and similar swing regions, voters expressed frustration at what they perceived as a national conversation focused more on cultural issues than on the economic pressures they faced daily, such as skyrocketing rent, stagnant wages, and medical costs (Associated Press, 2024). Analysts noted that the campaign's public alignment with celebrities and cultural influencers, rather than with working-class narratives and economic populism, alienated blue-collar voters already disillusioned with establishment politics (Reuters, 2024). Progressive commentators also criticized the campaign for appearing overly influenced by corporate advisors, arguing that this dulled the campaign's ability to connect with economically distressed voters who were seeking bold, transformative messaging (Jacobin, 2024).

In the end, while Winfrey's star power brought visibility, it also became a symbol of disconnect, illustrating how reliance on celebrity culture and elite endorsement can backfire when voters are seeking real-world solutions rather than red-carpet spectacles. These dynamics serve as a warning: when political campaigns tip too far toward symbolism, they risk losing the very voters they most need to win.

Case Study 3: Barack Obama and the Legacy of Leadership

Former President Barack Obama has long been a central figure in Democratic politics, widely respected for his eloquence, charisma, and ability to inspire across generations. During the 2024 presidential campaign, Obama emerged as a key surrogate for Vice President Kamala Harris, leveraging his enduring popularity to bolster her candidacy. Obama's speeches and public appearances sought to frame Harris as a continuation of his administration's legacy, highlighting shared values such as inclusivity, progressive reform, and the importance of strong, steady leadership in divisive times.

Obama's involvement energized Democratic voters, particularly among African Americans and younger progressives, who viewed his endorsement as a powerful call to action. However, his presence also drew criticism from conservatives and some independents, who argued that Obama's message often centered on idealism rather than addressing immediate economic concerns. In the Rust Belt states, where economic issues like job creation and inflation dominated the political conversation, Obama's focus on unity and long-term policy goals faced challenges in resonating with blue-collar voters.

Despite these hurdles, Obama's involvement proved instrumental in rallying urban and suburban voters. His ability to articulate a hopeful vision for the future, paired with his strong rapport with younger generations, helped mitigate some of the criticisms surrounding

Harris's campaign. However, as with many celebrity figures in politics, Obama's presence underscored the divide between progressive and working-class voters, highlighting the ongoing struggle for Democrats to balance idealism with practical economic solutions.

Case Study 4: Michelle Obama and the Power of Empathy

As one of the most admired figures in the United States, Michelle Obama brought a deeply personal and empathetic tone to her support for Kamala Harris during the 2024 election. Known for her authenticity and ability to connect with voters on a human level, Michelle focused her messaging on shared values, family, and the importance of perseverance in the face of adversity. Her "When We All Vote" initiative played a significant role in voter registration efforts, particularly among women, minorities, and first-time voters.

Michelle's advocacy for Harris resonated strongly with suburban women and younger voters, demographics critical to the Democratic coalition. Her speeches and media appearances emphasized Harris's historic candidacy, framing her as a symbol of progress and a leader uniquely qualified to address the challenges facing the nation. However, her involvement also faced backlash from conservative groups, who criticized her for emphasizing cultural and social issues over the economic concerns of working-class Americans.

Despite these critiques, Michelle's influence proved largely positive, elevating Harris's profile and energizing key segments of the Democratic base. Her ability to blend authenticity with a unifying message underscored her role as a bridge between progressive ideals and practical voter concerns. However, as with other celebrity endorsements, her impact highlighted the ongoing challenge of reaching voters who feel disconnected from the Democratic Party's broader platform.

Case Study 5: Bill Clinton and the Pragmatic Appeal

Former President Bill Clinton returned to the campaign trail in 2024, bringing with him a reputation for political pragmatism and his deep understanding of working-class concerns. Clinton's involvement was particularly focused on Rust Belt states, where he sought to reconnect with blue-collar voters who had drifted away from the Democratic Party in recent elections. His message centered on economic recovery, job creation, and rebuilding trust with communities that felt abandoned by national leadership.

While Clinton's charm and political acumen resonated with some older voters and union members, his presence also drew criticism. For younger and more progressive Democrats, Clinton represented an older era of compromise that some viewed as out of step with the party's current priorities. Additionally, his focus on economic issues occasionally clashed with the Harris campaign's emphasis on social progress and environmental reforms, creating a sense of dissonance within the broader Democratic message.

Nonetheless, Clinton's involvement demonstrated the enduring value of connecting with voters on economic issues. His ability to speak directly to the concerns of working-class Americans offered a glimpse of the strategies Democrats must adopt to rebuild trust with these critical constituencies.

Case Study 6: Beyoncé and the Power of Cultural Influence

Global icon Beyoncé once again took center stage during the 2024 election, using her immense cultural influence to advocate for Kamala Harris. Through high-profile performances, social media campaigns, and voter registration drives, Beyoncé energized younger voters and emphasized themes of empowerment and representation. Her efforts, particularly her focus on increasing turnout among Black voters and women, underscored the cultural significance of Harris's candidacy.

However, as with other celebrity endorsements, Beyoncé's involvement faced mixed reactions. While her advocacy was celebrated in urban centers and among progressive voters, critics in rural and conservative areas accused the Harris campaign of prioritizing celebrity endorsements over substantive policy proposals. For many working-class voters, Beyoncé's messaging on empowerment and social justice felt disconnected from their immediate economic concerns.

Despite these critiques, Beyoncé's influence cannot be understated. Her ability to command attention and inspire civic engagement brought national visibility to Harris's campaign, reinforcing the importance of representation and cultural leadership in modern politics. Yet, her involvement also underscored the challenges of bridging the divide between cultural influence and practical voter engagement in deeply divided electorates.

Case Study 7: LeBron James and Grassroots Mobilization

NBA superstar LeBron James expanded his political activism in 2024, using his platform to support Kamala Harris's campaign and encourage voter participation. Through his "More Than a Vote" initiative, James focused on combating voter suppression and increasing turnout among minorities and younger voters. His grassroots efforts, including funding polling stations and organizing community events, highlighted his commitment to empowering disenfranchised communities.

While James's activism was widely celebrated in urban areas, his involvement also sparked backlash from conservative commentators and some independents. Critics framed him as emblematic of Hollywood-style politics, arguing that his focus on social justice issues overshadowed the economic concerns of working-class voters. This critique was particularly pronounced in battleground states, where voters expressed frustration at what they perceived as an over-reliance on celebrity endorsements.

Despite these challenges, his influence was significant in mobilizing key voter blocs. His dedication to addressing systemic barriers to voting and his ability to connect with younger audiences brought energy and visibility to Harris's campaign. However, his involvement also highlighted the limitations of celebrity endorsements in regions where cultural and economic divides remain stark.

Case Study 8: Oprah Winfrey and the Harris Campaign

Oprah Winfrey, a media mogul and one of America's most influential cultural icons, brought her star power to Kamala Harris's 2024 presidential campaign, focusing on issues like healthcare equity, racial justice, and women's empowerment. Her passionate speeches and high-profile appearances drew attention to the Democratic platform, particularly among women, minorities, and urban voters. Through her "When We All Vote" initiative, Winfrey played a key role in voter registration and mobilization, adding weight to Harris's candidacy.

Winfrey's involvement generated excitement and media buzz but also faced sharp criticism, especially from conservative and working-class voters. For many, her immense wealth and celebrity status symbolized the Democratic Party's reliance on cultural elites. In battleground states like Pennsylvania and Ohio, voters viewed her focus on progressive social causes as they are blind to the real issues economic struggles, such as inflation and job security. Republican opponents seized on her presence to frame Harris's campaign as elitist and detached from middle America.

One notable moment was a star-studded town hall event in Georgia, organized by Winfrey's production company for $2.5 million. While it energized the Democratic base, the extravagance of the event drew backlash for appearing tone-deaf to voters grappling with economic challenges. Critics argued that Winfrey's messaging often overshadowed Harris's policy proposals, leaving key economic concerns unaddressed. This dynamic frustrated swing-state voters, who felt sidelined in favor of urban and progressive audiences.

Case Study 9: The View and the Illusion of Influence

Few platforms illustrate the celebrity echo chamber more vividly than The View, a long-running daytime talk show where media personalities, former celebrities, and political commentators convene to discuss current events, culture, and politics. With millions of viewers and a loyal following among progressive-leaning audiences, the show has become a soapbox for ultra-liberal commentary delivered with unwavering conviction. But behind the glamorous set and carefully curated hot topics lies a glaring disconnect: the cast members of The View are among the wealthiest women in entertainment, and their political advocacy is often insulated from the everyday struggles of the viewers they seek to influence.

The cast, featuring figures such as Whoopi Goldberg, Joy Behar, and Sunny Hostin, frequently engage in political discussions with the confidence of seasoned policymakers, despite lacking the policy expertise or lived experience to back it up. From sweeping declarations about healthcare and climate change to fiery condemnations of political opponents, their commentary often reflects the prevailing narratives of elite coastal liberalism. Yet, these narratives rarely speak to the economic and cultural concerns of working- and middle-class Americans. For many viewers outside the show's ideological bubble, The View comes off not as an enlightening dialogue but as a group of multimillionaires lecturing the public on how they should think, vote, and feel.

This illusion of influence is further amplified by the show's assumption that celebrity status grants political credibility. Cast members routinely engage in performative activism—championing causes they are often far removed from, while offering little in the way of practical solutions. When discussing issues like inflation, housing insecurity, or the cost of living, their perspectives are filtered through a lens of immense privilege. It's difficult to take economic advice seriously from someone whose weekly paycheck dwarfs the annual income of most Americans.

The show's hyper-liberal tone and dismissive attitude toward dissenting viewpoints have alienated large swaths of the electorate. In swing states and rural regions, The View has become a punchline, a symbol of how out-of-touch liberal elites have become with the people they claim to represent. Critics argue that the cast's narrow worldview and monolithic political leanings foster groupthink rather than genuine dialogue. The assumption that progressive ideology is the only "correct" stance not only undermines political pluralism but reinforces the public's growing resentment toward celebrity-driven politics.

Despite their media reach, the cast of The View consistently overestimates their ability to shape public opinion. Rather than persuading undecided voters, their rhetoric often hardens partisan divisions and fuels cultural resentment. What's presented as a spirited defense of democracy and justice is often perceived by working-class viewers as elitism masquerading as moral authority.

Ultimately, The View serves as a cautionary tale of what happens when celebrity voices mistake visibility for wisdom and wealth for relatability. In a political climate demanding empathy, nuance, and authenticity, the show offers none, and reminds us that loud voices from ivory towers rarely echo in the hearts of ordinary Americans.

The Broader Implications of the Celebrity Trap

The over-reliance on celebrity endorsements highlights a deeper challenge within modern political campaigns: the prioritization of image over substance. In an era dominated by viral moments and social media engagement, the allure of celebrity involvement often supersedes the need for meaningful policy discussions. While celebrities can draw massive attention to a campaign, generating headlines and amplifying messages to millions of followers, their presence frequently overshadows the critical issues at the heart of the political agenda. For voters grappling with tangible concerns like inflation, job insecurity, housing affordability, and healthcare access, the focus on star power feels clueless and disconnected from their lived experiences. This creates a growing gap between campaign strategies and the real-world struggles of constituents.

This image-first approach reflects a broader cultural shift in politics, one where the performance of leadership outweighs the practice of it. Voters increasingly view campaigns as spectacles orchestrated for public relations gains rather than forums for substantive dialogue. This spectacle breeds cynicism, particularly among middle- and working-class Americans, who see political elites courting celebrities instead of crafting policies that address their economic realities and safety concerns (Pew Research Center, 2023).

The use of celebrities as political surrogates also risks deepening social and cultural divides. High-profile endorsements tend to resonate most with urban, younger, and progressive audience groups already aligned with the values often espoused by celebrity advocates. But this approach alienates rural and working-class voters, who view such endorsements as yet another symbol of cultural elitism. Many of these voters feel excluded not only by the campaigns themselves, but by the celebrities who, from their mansions and gated studios, claim to speak for the common person. The result is a growing perception that political elites care more about gaining the approval of Hollywood than understanding the people they claim to represent.

While celebrities excel at commanding attention and shaping narratives in entertainment, their foray into politics frequently reveals the limits of their influence. Their expertise lies in performing, not policymaking, and their attempts to weigh in on complex political matters often highlight a lack of depth and understanding. During the 2024 presidential campaign, numerous celebrities lent their voices to political causes, but their involvement more often than not ended in embarrassment. Their messages were misaligned with the real concerns of voters or overshadowed by personal controversies. Instead of strengthening campaigns, these endorsements became distractions that derailed meaningful conversations about the issues that matter.

This phenomenon also reflects a broader cultural delusion, many celebrities believe that their fame and visibility grant them automatic authority in political discourse. Yet voters increasingly view these interventions as self-serving and out of touch, further diminishing the effectiveness of star-powered endorsements. Rather than elevating a campaign, celebrity involvement often results in missteps that undermine the very causes they claim to support.

To bridge this divide, political campaigns must take a more thoughtful approach to celebrity involvement. Endorsements should never be treated as substitutes for grassroots engagement. Instead, they should strategically complement policy-driven messaging. If celebrities are brought in, their values must align with the campaign's target audience, and their connection to the issue should be genuine, whether through personal experience or professional credibility. For example, a celebrity advocating for healthcare reform should have a meaningful connection to that cause, not simply a PR contract.

Authenticity is essential. Voters are increasingly skeptical of endorsements that feel staged or opportunistic. Campaigns must ensure that celebrity advocates are genuinely committed and can communicate goals effectively. More importantly, they must balance star power with substantive outreach, town halls, policy briefings, community forums. These efforts show a commitment to listening to voters and prioritizing their voices over the optics of celebrity spectacle.

By aligning celebrity voices with the real values and concerns of their constituents, and using them to complement, not eclipse, substantive engagement, political leaders can tap into cultural influence without falling into the celebrity trap. Meanwhile, celebrities should recognize their limits. Their greatest contributions may still lie in entertainment, impersonating fictional characters or singing songs written by others, not in shaping public policy. Staying in their lane would save them from embarrassment and protect the very causes they claim to support from their unintended sabotage.

When Celebrity Politics Misses the Mark

The 2024 presidential campaign was a masterclass in how over-reliance on celebrities can derail political efforts, turning what could have been strategic advantages into liabilities. From Barack Obama's idealistic but disconnected speeches to Michelle Obama's heartfelt yet divisive advocacy, and from Taylor Swift's polarizing social media campaigns to Oprah Winfrey's star-studded yet out of step with reality during here events, the campaign inadvertently spotlighted the pitfalls of leaning too heavily on star power. While these figures undoubtedly brought visibility and energy to Kamala Harris's campaign, they also exposed a glaring disconnect between the cultural elite and the everyday struggles of American voters.

In battleground states, voters burdened by inflation, healthcare costs, and job insecurity saw the celebrity-fueled campaign as emblematic of a broader detachment from their realities. Beyoncé's empowerment messaging felt distant to those living paycheck to paycheck, while LeBron James's calls for social justice appeared to sideline the economic concerns of working families. Oprah's town halls reinforced perceptions of elitism, and even Bill Clinton, once known for his blue-collar appeal, struggled to break through the fog of spectacle and reconnect with disillusioned voters.

What unified these endorsements, whether it was Swift singing progressive anthems from a Manhattan penthouse, James offering voter advice between luxury brand deals, or the cast of *The View* pontificating from a studio far removed from the average American's world, was a shared delusion: the belief that fame equates to political authority. These celebrities, cocooned in privilege, seemed convinced that their stardom granted them not just insight into public life, but the power to shape it. They mistook applause for policy credibility and visibility for voter connection. From Obama's soaring rhetoric to Oprah's lavish showcases, the whole affair resembled a telethon for elite validation rather than a movement grounded in the struggles of real people.

Nowhere was this disconnect more glaring than in the conduct of these ultra-wealthy surrogates, who genuinely believed that their names alone could sway elections. But everyday voters, juggling rent, gas, childcare, and shrinking paychecks, saw not champions, but clueless elites. For all their rehearsed empathy and camera-ready speeches, these figures failed to grasp the most basic truth: Americans don't want to be lectured by people who've never had to stretch a dollar or skip a medical bill. These celebrities would be wise to return to what they do best, portraying fictional characters or performing songs someone else wrote—rather than assuming they speak for millions whose lives they cannot begin to understand.

The celebrity surrogates and former leaders who rallied for Harris did more than amplify her platform, they became distractions. Their missteps, tone-deaf statements, and high-profile appearances often eclipsed the policies they were supposed to promote. From awkward gaffes to elitist optics, their presence revealed the fundamental danger in confusing popularity with political legitimacy.

In the end, the Democratic Party's over-reliance on cultural icons alienated the very voters it needed most. It tarnished the campaign's image of authenticity, reinforced perceptions of elitism, and weakened the connection between candidate and constituent. The lesson is clear: real political power doesn't come from red carpets or viral moments, it comes from showing up, listening, and connecting with the people who cast the votes.

Chapter 6

Failing to Engage the Working Class

For much of the 20th century, the Democratic Party was the unwavering ally of America's working class, championing labor unions, industrial growth, and blue-collar economic security. Yet, in recent decades, this bond has frayed, leaving many working-class voters feeling abandoned by a party increasingly focused on urban progressivism and cultural activism. The erosion of this once-solid alliance has had profound consequences, particularly in the industrial Midwest and Rust Belt states that were the backbone of the party's electoral strength. The decline of union power, the rise of globalization, and a widening cultural disconnect have driven many blue-collar voters to seek political refuge elsewhere, particularly among Republican candidates who promise to protect traditional industries and champion "America First" policies. As the Democratic Party continues to pivot toward progressive social reforms and climate initiatives, its failure to address the immediate economic concerns of working-class Americans threatens not only its historical base but also its future viability as the party of labor and opportunity.

The Erosion of the Democratic Party's Blue-Collar Base

For much of the 20th century, the Democratic Party was synonymous with the working class. Labor unions, manufacturing hubs, and blue-collar voters were the foundation of the party's political strength, particularly in industrial states like Michigan, Pennsylvania, and Ohio. However, in recent decades, this traditional alliance has eroded, leaving many working-class voters feeling abandoned by a party that once championed their economic concerns. This shift has had profound electoral consequences, as the Democratic Party struggles to retain its historical base while addressing the diverse needs of an increasingly fragmented electorate.

The erosion of the blue-collar base can be traced to several factors. First, the decline of manufacturing in the United States has decimated union membership and weakened organized labor, long a cornerstone of Democratic support. Between 1980 and 2020, union membership in the private sector fell from 20% to just 6%, leaving fewer institutions to mobilize working-class voters around Democratic platforms (AFL-CIO, 2023). The Democratic Party's pivot toward progressive social policies and environmental reforms, while resonating with urban and younger voters, has alienated many in the industrial heartland who view these policies as threats to their jobs and way of life (Wood and Herbst, 2007).

For example, initiatives aimed at combating climate change, such as transitioning to renewable energy and phasing out fossil fuels, have sparked resistance among workers in industries like coal mining, oil drilling, and auto manufacturing. While these policies align with long-term environmental goals, they are often seen as dismissive of the economic realities facing workers in these sectors. It was found that in key battleground states, this perception has driven a significant number of blue-collar voters toward Republican candidates who promise to protect traditional industries and "put America first" (Larsson, 2021).

Moreover, the cultural divide between the Democratic Party and the working class has widened. Many blue-collar voters perceive the party's focus on progressive social issues, such as gender politics and racial equity, as disconnected from their daily struggles. While these issues are important, their prominence in Democratic messaging often overshadows kitchen-table concerns like wages, healthcare, and job security. This misalignment has fueled the perception that the party is more concerned with urban elites and cultural influencers than with the needs of rural and industrial communities (Cinelli et al., 2023; Fair Elections Center, 2023; Primerica, 2023; The Guardian, 2023).

Missteps in the Midwest and Rust Belt

The Democratic Party's challenges in engaging the working class have been particularly pronounced in battleground states like Michigan, Wisconsin, and Pennsylvania, areas where blue-collar voters have historically played a decisive role in shaping electoral outcomes. These states, often referred to collectively as the Rust Belt, were once Democratic strongholds due to their dense populations of unionized factory workers and laborers. However, recent elections have exposed a troubling trend: many of these voters are shifting their allegiance to Republican candidates who emphasize economic nationalism, traditional values, and cultural conservatism. The erosion of Democratic support in these regions underscores a critical vulnerability in the party's electoral strategy.

One of the most glaring missteps has been the Democratic Party's inability to adequately address the economic anxieties of Rust Belt voters. For decades, these communities have borne the brunt of globalization, automation, and the decline of American manufacturing. Factories that once provided stable, well-paying jobs have shuttered, leaving entire towns grappling with unemployment, reduced tax bases, and deteriorating infrastructure. Despite these challenges, Democratic messaging in these states has often prioritized progressive social policies over the immediate economic recovery that many voters seek. The party's focus on issues like healthcare reform, climate action, and racial equity, while important, has often failed to resonate with working-class voters whose primary concerns center on wages, job security, and economic revitalization.

This misalignment was starkly evident in the 2016 presidential election. Hillary Clinton's campaign, which leaned heavily on a progressive platform, failed to connect with blue-collar voters in Michigan and Wisconsin. These narrow but pivotal losses underscored the Democrats' inability to effectively address the bread-and-butter economic issues that dominate Rust Belt households (Wood and Herbst, 2007). Clinton's comments about phasing out coal jobs and her perceived detachment from the struggles of industrial communities provided a stark contrast to Donald Trump's promises to "bring back jobs" and revive American manufacturing. This dynamic led many Rust Belt voters, who had traditionally supported Democrats, to vote Republican or abstain altogether.

Authenticity Over Optics

The 2024 presidential campaign echoed many of these same challenges. Vice President Kamala Harris's platform focused on progressive policies like climate action, healthcare reform, and social justice. While these issues resonated with younger, urban, and coastal voters, they often failed to address the economic realities of the Midwest. Harris's support for transitioning away from fossil fuels and increasing regulations on traditional industries was framed by Republican opponents as a direct attack on the livelihoods of workers in manufacturing, coal, and energy sectors. In battleground states like Ohio and Pennsylvania, Republican messaging struck a chord by emphasizing job creation, energy independence, and protecting traditional industries. This strategy appeals strongly to blue-collar voters who felt their concerns were being overlooked by the Democratic Party's national platform for decades (Larsson, 2021).

Compounding these challenges was the Democratic Party's lack of an effective ground game in Rust Belt communities. Unlike their

Republican counterparts, who often employed targeted outreach strategies in rural and industrial areas, Democrats were criticized for focusing their resources on urban centers and suburban districts. This imbalance left many working-class voters feeling ignored and undervalued. For example, in Pennsylvania, voters in small towns expressed frustration that campaign events and resources were concentrated in Philadelphia and Pittsburgh, while rural and industrial areas were largely neglected. This perceived neglect fueled a narrative that the Democratic Party is disconnected from reality and the needs of working-class Americans.

This sense of detachment was further exacerbated by the party's reliance on high-profile endorsements from celebrities and cultural elites. While these endorsements energized segments of the Democratic base, particularly younger and progressive voters, they alienated many working-class voters in the Rust Belt. For individuals grappling with rising costs of living and job insecurity, the involvement of celebrities often felt disconnected from their day-to-day struggles. The sight of Hollywood actors and pop stars rallying for Democratic candidates only deepened the perception that the party was prioritizing image over substance, catering to cultural elites rather than the "forgotten Americans" who had once formed the backbone of their coalition (Cinelli et al., 2023; Fair Elections Center, 2023; Primerica, 2023; The Guardian, 2023).

To regain lost ground in the Midwest and Rust Belt, the Democratic Party must prioritize addressing the economic concerns of blue-collar voters. Policies aimed at revitalizing manufacturing, investing in infrastructure, and creating sustainable job opportunities are essential to rebuilding trust with these communities. Moreover, the party must adopt a more inclusive messaging strategy that balances its progressive values with the immediate needs of working-class voters. This involves framing climate policies as opportunities for economic growth, such as emphasizing job creation in clean energy industries, rather than as threats to traditional livelihoods.

Additionally, the party must invest in grassroots organizing and outreach in Rust Belt communities. Establishing a strong presence in small towns and industrial hubs, listening to the concerns of voters, and tailoring policies to reflect their needs can help bridge the cultural divide that has alienated these regions. By focusing on empathy, practicality, and engagement, the Democratic Party can begin to repair its relationship with the working class and reclaim its historical standing as the party of labor and economic opportunity. Without such efforts, the Rust Belt and Midwest may continue to drift further from the Democratic coalition, with lasting consequences for the party's national prospects.

Rebuilding the Relationship with the Working Class

Re-engaging the working-class base will require the Democratic Party to undergo a fundamental recalibration of its messaging and policy priorities. Historically, the party has been most successful when it positioned itself as the champion of labor rights and economic equity, a legacy it must rekindle to win back the trust of blue-collar voters. To achieve this, Democrats must shift their focus toward addressing the immediate economic concerns of these communities while maintaining their broader progressive vision.

Prioritizing Economic Issues

First and foremost, the Democratic Party must place a renewed emphasis on economic issues that directly impact blue-collar voters. Policies aimed at creating jobs, investing in infrastructure, and ensuring affordable healthcare should take center stage, especially in battleground states like Michigan, Wisconsin, and Pennsylvania. Job creation policies should be specific, actionable, and localized, addressing the unique needs of the Rust Belt communities. For example, federal investments in rebuilding decaying infrastructure, such as roads, bridges, and water systems, would not only provide employment opportunities but also demonstrate a tangible commitment to improving the quality of life in these areas.

Moreover, addressing healthcare affordability remains a critical issue for working-class voters. Proposals to reduce prescription drug prices, expand Medicaid, and protect workers' access to employer-sponsored health insurance must be central to the Democratic platform. These policies should be communicated in ways that resonate with the lived experiences of voters, framing them as not only reforms but lifelines for families struggling to balance medical costs with other essential expenses.

Additionally, Democrats need to articulate clear strategies for mitigating the economic impacts of globalization and technological change. For decades, globalization has contributed to job losses in manufacturing-heavy regions, while automation continues to displace workers across industries. Addressing these challenges will require innovative policy solutions, such as tax incentives for companies that create domestic manufacturing jobs, support for unionization efforts, and workforce retraining programs that equip workers with the skills needed for emerging industries.

Running a firm in the environmental sector, I couldn't find trained specialists—not because the talent wasn't out there, but because workforce pipelines were built around bureaucratic optics, not market needs. That disconnect between education systems and job readiness is a glaring example of how out-of-touch political planning can sabotage real opportunity. It's not enough to talk about job creation, we must build the bridges between ambition and execution, between talent and employment.

Even in higher education, building these pipelines is a battle. As a college dean overseeing workforce programs, I witnessed firsthand how difficult it was to align education with industry demands. Why? Because federal funding, state policy, and institutional direction were all filtered through layers of political bureaucracy, often party-driven and detached from real-world outcomes. The trickle-down effect was poor at best, leaving students with credentials that sounded good on paper but didn't translate into job offers. When politics leads and practicality lags, it's the students, and the future workforce, who pay the price.

Bridging the Cultural Divide

The Democratic Party must also confront the growing cultural divide that has alienated many working-class voters. In recent years, the party's focus on progressive social policies, while vital, has sometimes been perceived as prioritizing urban and elite concerns over the day-to-day struggles of industrial and rural communities. To rebuild trust, Democrats must adopt a rhetoric that emphasizes shared values and common goals rather than divisive language that can exacerbate cultural tensions.

This shift involves framing policies in terms of their universal benefits. For example, instead of focusing solely on the environmental benefits of transitioning to clean energy, Democrats could emphasize how such a transition would create well-paying, sustainable jobs in regions traditionally reliant on coal, oil, or manufacturing. By presenting these policies as solutions that protect both livelihoods and the environment, the party can appeal to a broader coalition of voters.

Grassroots engagement will be critical in bridging this divide. Democrats must invest in on-the-ground organizing efforts, ensuring that campaign resources are allocated to rural and industrial areas often overlooked by national political strategies. Establishing a consistent presence in these communities, through town halls, listening sessions, and local partnerships, can help rebuild trust and relationships. Moreover, actively listening to the concerns of working-class voters and incorporating their perspectives into the party platform will demonstrate a genuine commitment to addressing their needs.

Balancing Progressivism with Economic Realities

Finally, the Democratic Party must find a way to balance its progressive agenda with the economic realities of industrial and rural communities. This means crafting policies that address climate change, social justice, and other key issues without alienating voters who rely on traditional industries for their livelihoods.

For example, climate change policies must go beyond aspirational goals to include pragmatic solutions that protect and support workers in fossil fuel-dependent industries. This could involve establishing federal programs that retrain coal miners and oil workers for jobs in renewable energy, offering financial assistance during career transitions, and ensuring that clean energy projects are located in regions most affected by the decline of traditional industries. Such programs would send a clear message that the Democratic Party values workers' contributions and is committed to their economic security during periods of transition.

Similarly, social justice initiatives must be framed in ways that resonate with the broader electorate. Instead of focusing solely on specific demographic groups, Democrats should emphasize how these policies benefit society as a whole. For example, criminal justice reform can be presented as a way to enhance public safety and economic stability for all communities, regardless of their demographic makeup.

By focusing on pragmatic, inclusive solutions, the Democratic Party can demonstrate that its policies are not just aspirational but also attainable. The goal should be to craft a platform that respects the values and economic realities of working-class voters while advancing a progressive vision for the future. This balancing act will require thoughtful messaging, careful policy design, and a renewed commitment to engaging with voters where they are.

Rebuilding the working-class base will not happen overnight, but with consistent effort, empathy, and a focus on economic and cultural inclusivity, the Democratic Party can begin to restore its reputation as the party of the people. Only by addressing the concerns of all Americans, regardless of geography or occupation, can the party forge a path forward that is both politically viable and true to its historical roots.

The Democratic Party's over-reliance on celebrity endorsements has exposed a fundamental flaw in modern political strategy: the prioritization of spectacle over substance. While celebrities may command attention and generate excitement, their involvement often reveals a disconnect between campaign priorities and the concerns of everyday Americans. The 2024 election starkly highlighted this miscalculation, as the overinflated self-image of many celebrities was laid bare for all to see. Their attempts to influence voters often came across as tone-deaf, self-serving, and detached from the realities of working-class and rural Americans. Rather than galvanizing support, these endorsements frequently alienated critical voter blocs, reinforcing the perception that the party was more focused on appeasing cultural elites than addressing the struggles of ordinary citizens. By leaning so heavily on figures who mistake fame for credibility, the Democratic Party undermined its ability to connect with voters on meaningful issues. The lesson is clear: campaigns must return to the fundamentals of grassroots engagement, policy-driven messaging, and authentic leadership, leaving the celebrities to entertain rather than govern.

Chapter 7

Both Parties Are Spending America into Collapse

America's national debt is not a partisan problem. It's a bipartisan betrayal, a quiet, relentless erosion of our nation's future, fed by Democrats and Republicans alike. While they argue on cable news and fundraise off their supposed differences, both parties have been united in one fundamental truth: they win elections by spending your money, not saving it. They trade long-term solvency for short-term political gain, and in doing so, they are writing the downfall of a superpower.

As of 2025, the United States' national debt has surpassed $36 trillion, a staggering number that defies comprehension. To grasp the sheer insanity of $36 trillion in debt, let's break it down. That's over $109,000 for every man, woman, and child in the United States, and that's before interest. Imagine handing a newborn baby a bill the size of a luxury car and telling them, "Good luck, kid." That's not a metaphor. That's the reality we're in. Now multiply that by every child in your family, every neighbor on your street, every worker at your job, and ask yourself: how long can any empire survive when its citizens are born into chains of debt they never agreed to carry? This isn't just a national liability, it's a generational sentence. Every dollar borrowed is a dollar stolen from your future, your children's freedom, and your grandchildren's opportunities. Rome didn't fall because it lacked culture. It fell because it couldn't balance a ledger. America is racing down that same road—with a smile on its face and a credit card in its hand.

Yet Congress continues to pass trillion-dollar budgets, each side claiming moral justification for their spending spree. The left calls it "investing in the future." The right calls it "defending freedom." In reality, they're both bankrupting the country, just wearing different colors while they do it.

The Myth of Fiscal Responsibility

Democrats promise sweeping social programs, student loan forgiveness, and green energy initiatives, mall funded with borrowed money. Republicans demand tax cuts, defense build-ups, and border walls, also funded with borrowed money. Each claims to be fiscally responsible. Neither is. The last time the U.S. federal government ran a surplus was in 2001. Since then, every president, Bush, Obama, Trump, and Biden, has added to the debt. And the party in power always finds a way to justify it.

Even worse, neither party seems to have any real intention of paying the debt down. Budget "cuts" are often just reductions in projected increases. Debt ceiling debates are political theater, inevitably ending with more borrowing, followed by both sides patting themselves on the back for having reached a so-called "compromise." But make no mistake: they are compromising your children's future.

I've written grants that had to navigate 80 pages of red tape just to fund basic STEM labs, while watching billions disappear into political pork. That kind of hypocrisy isn't just inefficient; it's demoralizing. It's a betrayal of those who still believe government can be a force for good, for real solutions and real futures.

Early in my career, while working for a legacy environmental firm, I saw the U.S. EPA push through projects that served no real purpose, just to spend down budgets before the fiscal year ended. These weren't infrastructure upgrades or community reinvestments. They were bureaucratic exercise studies no one read, reports that sat on shelves, projects designed to look productive on paper. Meanwhile, in higher education, students go without functioning lab equipment, without access to the tools required to master the hard sciences. In public K–12 classrooms, kids still share outdated textbooks and photocopied handouts.

And yet, politicians on both sides of the aisle, Democrats and Republicans alike, never seem to have trouble funding their pet projects. Take, for example, $1 million spent on a neon sign museum in Las Vegas (Taxpayers for Common Sense, 2012), $8 million wasted on a "green" bus stop in Arlington, Virginia—one that cost more than the buses themselves (Barrett, 2013), and $2 million used to upgrade an unused desert airstrip that conveniently benefited a major political donor's property (Schulte, 2014). These aren't one-offs. They're symptoms of a deeply broken political culture, where pork-barrel projects are prioritized over public needs.

While Americans ration insulin, drown in student debt, and sit in overcrowded classrooms, their elected leaders are funding ghost airports and vanity museums. This isn't just mismanagement, it's bipartisan betrayal. It's political vanity, paid for by a taxpayer base that gets less with every election cycle.

A Lesson from Fallen Empires

History has seen this story before, and it rarely ends well. Rome, once the greatest empire in the Western world, didn't collapse overnight. It crumbled from within. Crippling debt, debased currency, political corruption, and unsustainable military spending drained its strength. But perhaps most importantly, the ruling elite lost touch with the everyday Roman. While senators dined in luxury and debated over palace politics, ordinary citizens struggled with inflation, unemployment, and civil unrest. That disconnect, between the governed and those who claimed to govern, proved fatal.

Fast forward to the 21st century, and Greece faced a modern-day reckoning. After decades of irresponsible borrowing, bloated government programs, and political promises that far outpaced economic productivity, the country was forced into humiliating austerity. Riots filled the streets. Pensions were slashed. The working class paid the price for elite mismanagement, as global creditors stripped the nation of its autonomy.

Even the United Kingdom, once the dominant global empire, saw its stature slowly eroded, not just by the cost of two world wars, but by the unsustainable expansion of its welfare state and failure to modernize its economy. Britain didn't fall in flames; it quietly declined into something smaller, less ambitious, and more fragile.

And then there's the USSR, a superpower brought to its knees not by bombs, but by economic rot. The Soviet elite poured money into military expansion, bloated social programs, and rigid bureaucracies with little oversight or accountability. They ignored the mounting dysfunction across rural and industrial regions, lied about economic conditions, and clung to ideological narratives while their people lined up for bread. The collapse was sudden, but the decay was slow and deliberate. By the time the leadership noticed the crisis, it was already too late.

America is not immune. We are not "too big to fail." When the political class becomes so insulated by wealth, ideology, and power that it can no longer see or feel the struggles of ordinary Americans, collapse is not just possible, it is inevitable. The debt we carry is not theoretical. It's a loaded weapon pointed at the future. Every borrowed dollar must be repaid, refinanced, or defaulted. Interest payments on the debt are now one of the fastest-growing expenses in the federal budget, projected to surpass even defense spending in the next decade.

At some point, lenders will lose confidence. At some point, the world will question the dollar's reliability. At some point, the entire system, propped up by illusion and inertia, will break.

And when it does, it won't be the politicians or the billionaires who suffer. It will be the working class. The teachers, the truck drivers, the single mothers, the veterans. It will be the people who were ignored for decades while their leaders smiled for cameras, posted soundbites, and passed trillion-dollar budgets they knew we could never afford.

History is not just warning us. It's daring us to keep pretending this time is different. But history always wins.

Why Keep Spending

Why do both parties keep doing this? Because buying votes works. It's not about responsible governance anymore, it's about political survival. Promising free healthcare, student loan relief, child tax credits, stimulus checks, or trillion-dollar infrastructure projects makes for great headlines and catchy campaign ads. It fires up the base, manipulates the media narrative, and gives voters just enough hope, or just enough cash, to feel like someone in Washington is doing something for them. It's not policymaking, it's bribery with a patriotic label.

Telling the American people the hard truth, that we need to cut spending, raise taxes, or reform entitlements, is political suicide. No one wants to be the adult in the room when the rest of Congress is throwing money out the windows like its Monopoly cash. So, what do they do? They lie. They inflate. They borrow. And then they get re-elected.

But the recklessness doesn't stop at the federal level. Look at state, county, and municipal governments, where the same dangerous habits are playing out on a smaller scale. One of the biggest silent killers of fiscal solvency is the expansion of government pension promises made by elected officials who knew they wouldn't be in office when the bill came due. These pensions, once seen as sacred and secure, are now bleeding budgets dry. In many states, public pensions are paying out far more than they take in, with future obligations vastly exceeding current assets.

Cities like Detroit, Stockton, and San Bernardino have already declared bankruptcy, in part due to pension obligations they couldn't meet. Illinois teeters on the edge of fiscal collapse with one of the worst-funded pension systems in the country, while states like New Jersey and Connecticut carry enormous liabilities they've repeatedly failed to address. Even wealthier states have resorted to borrowing, restructuring, or quietly cutting benefits to stay afloat. What was once a pillar of government employment guaranteed pension for decades of service, is now a burden that threatens to collapse the system itself.

This is not just a federal issue. This is a nationwide epidemic of over-promising and under-delivering, enabled by politicians at every level who buy favor today with money tomorrow. And like every pyramid scheme, it works until it doesn't. When the economic pressure mounts, when tax revenues dip, when inflation spikes, or when investment returns fall short, the whole structure begins to crumble.

Both parties are addicted to spending, and like any addict, they'll deny they have a problem right up until the overdose. The difference? When Congress, state legislatures, and city councils' overdose on debt and obligations, it's the taxpayers and retirees who suffer. The average American faces higher taxes, fewer services, and the gut-wrenching possibility that the retirement system they counted on, federal or local, may not be there when they need it most.

There is no "party of fiscal responsibility" anymore. The old conservative promise of balanced budgets is dead. The progressive pledge of economic justice now depends on infinite credit. What we're left with is a system where both sides are selling you the future in exchange for their political present. There's no left or right, just spenders in red ties and spenders in blue suits, and neither has a serious plan to pay the tab.

This isn't governance. It's short-termism on steroids, a never-ending campaign cycle where winning is the only metric that matters. And when winning means spending your money, printing more of it, and making promises that outlive their makers, what you get isn't democracy. What you get is collapse disguised as progress.

A Ponzi Scheme in Red, White, and Blue

Our elected officials have perfected the political trifecta of economic delusion: cut taxes, increase spending, and pray it all works out. It's the fiscal equivalent of eating cake for every meal and hoping your grandkids go on a diet. The promises are always the same: You'll pay less, get more, and somehow, miraculously, it will all balance out. But it never does.

The math isn't just fuzzy, it's fraudulent. Politicians campaign like Santa Claus and govern like gamblers, handing out goodies they know we can't afford while pretending the debt will magically vanish if we just "grow the economy" fast enough.

They offer tax cuts without offsets, benefits without budgets, and stimulus without strategy. It's a political sugar high, great in the moment, catastrophic in the long run. They sell dreams backed by debt, bribe voters with borrowed money, and then hand the bill to someone who hasn't even been born yet. There's no accountability, no adult in the room, just career politicians auctioning off the future in exchange for applause today.

And we, the voters, fall for it. Every. Single. Time. We cheer for the lies because they're comfortable. Because it feels good to be promised everything and asked for nothing. Because being told we can have prosperity without sacrifice is the most seductive fiction ever told in a democracy. But reality doesn't care about applause lines.

Just look at 2007 and 2008, a masterclass in financial denial and consequences. Americans were living large on money they didn't have, buying homes they couldn't afford, while banks repackaged junk debt into "safe" investments and sold it to the world. It all looked brilliant, until it collapsed. Trillions in wealth vanished. Retirement accounts were obliterated. Families lost homes, jobs, and futures. It was the worst economic crash since the Great Depression, and it was caused by the same delusional thinking we still cling to today: we can borrow, spend, and fake our way through it. But we can't. And next time, it won't just be Wall Street on fire, it'll be Washington, pensions, the dollar itself.

This isn't governance. It's cowardice wrapped in charisma. This isn't strategy. It's sabotage with a smile. And it's not leadership, it's a Ponzi scheme wearing a flag pin, counting on your short memory, your misplaced trust, and your willingness to believe that someone else will deal with it later.

Only they won't.

Meanwhile, the Elites Get Richer

But here's the gut punch: economic collapse doesn't hurt everyone equally. In fact, for the ultra-wealthy and celebrities, crisis often means opportunity. When inflation surges and the stock market dips, the average American sees their savings erode, their rent rise, and their grocery bills balloon. The average American is too busy surviving while the rich are buying stocks. Billionaire class swoop in, buy up distressed assets, capitalize on market volatility, and expand their wealth.

Just look at what happened during the COVID-19 recession. While millions of Americans lost jobs and small businesses shuttered, billionaires added trillions of dollars to their net worth. During periods of economic pain, the ultra-rich get richer, and celebrities keep cashing checks, selling access, and maintaining influence. The economy collapses, but their brand value explodes. Endorsements, appearances, political consulting gigs; they all profit from chaos.

In a debt-driven collapse, Wall Street has hedges. The wealthy have tax shelters. Celebrities have contracts and clout. But Main Street? It has none of that. Working families face layoffs. Seniors lose retirement value. Young people see homeownership slip further away. And both political parties will look around, like they always do, and say, "No one saw it coming."

A Nation in Denial

America has become a nation in denial. We look away because the debt doesn't hit us immediately. There's no siren blaring when Congress adds another trillion to the national tab. There's no instant collapse when interest rates creep upward or when inflation quietly eats away at our paychecks. Instead, we're lulled into a false sense of security by the illusion of stability, a carefully crafted mirage supported by media soundbites, government spin, and the one thing that numbs the pain: access to easy credit.

And the ruling class knows it. They know that as long as the average American can still swipe a credit card, lease a new truck, or finance a kitchen remodel, they'll stay calm. They know that consumer confidence doesn't need to be grounded in reality, it just needs to be maintained long enough to win the next election. Give people enough distractions, keep them shopping, and most will ignore the slow-motion collapse happening right under their feet.

Meanwhile, the wealthy, political elites, and celebrities are playing a very different game. They see the writing on the wall. They have teams of financial advisors who are already telling them to hold cash, buy land, stockpile hard assets, and diversify into inflation-proof investments. They're preparing. Quietly. Strategically. Because they understand that when the collapse comes, and it will, they'll be the ones with liquidity, leverage, and real assets. They won't be surprised. They'll be positioned.

But the average American? They've were sold a lie. They've been taught that buying a luxury car, wearing designer clothes, or living beyond their means is a signal of success. In reality, it's a mask for pain and a symptom of denial. While the rich consolidate wealth and buy when the market dips, everyday people are buying to feel better, thinking their spending power today somehow protects them from what's coming tomorrow. It doesn't. It only makes the impact more brutal.

When the crash comes, it won't just be financial, it will be emotional. Millions will be blindsided. Jobs will vanish. Credit will dry up. Savings will be wiped out. People will look around and wonder how it all happened so fast. But the truth is, it didn't happen fast. It happened slowly, in plain sight, while we were binge-shopping, scrolling through influencer content, and believing that debt-fueled consumption was the same as wealth.

It was never the same. And when the illusion shatters, we'll find out who was preparing, and who was pretending.

Financial Collapse Is a Choice

This isn't about Democrats or Republicans anymore. This is about survival. About whether the United States continues as a functioning democracy or becomes the next cautionary tale whispered in future history classes. If we do not change course, and soon, we will join the ranks of once-great powers that fell not to foreign armies, but to self-inflicted rot, born of arrogance, denial, and unchecked indulgence.

Rome didn't fall in a day. Neither will we. But fall we will, if we continue to let our leaders spend recklessly, promise endlessly, and govern like gamblers in a casino with your children's future on the table. They know the system is broken. They just don't care, because they think they'll be gone before the bill comes due.

And while they argue over who to blame, while career politicians point fingers and celebrities' tweet about justice from behind the gates of multimillion-dollar estates, it's working Americans who will bear the burden. The truck driver. The schoolteacher. The factory worker. The single mom. The soldier. The small business owner. They will pay the price for a system built to enrich the few and placate the rest with credit cards and cheap slogans.

Let's be clear: collapse won't come with fireworks; it will come with silence. A bank account frozen. A pension cut in half. A currency worth less than the paper it's printed on. A generation locked out of opportunity, asking how we let it get this bad.

We are not entitled to a happy ending. We must choose it. The time has come for a national reckoning, a demand for truth over talking points, responsibility over re-election, and courage over comfort. Real reform. Real sacrifice. Real leadership.

Because collapse isn't fate. It's a choice.

Chapter 8

The Social Media Echo Chamber

The 2024 election cycle revealed the stark limitations of celebrity influence, media bias, and the weaponization of social media in modern politics. Despite the overwhelming backing of high-profile figures and glowing coverage from mainstream outlets, the Democratic Party faced a sobering reality: a disconnect between their strategies and the electorate's priorities. Celebrities, buoyed by their own inflated sense of importance, dominated headlines and social media feeds with endorsements that often-alienated key demographics rather than inspiring unity. Meanwhile, a media landscape heavily skewed toward progressive narratives failed to resonate with large swaths of voters who felt ignored or vilified. Social media platforms like Twitter, TikTok, and Instagram further compounded these challenges by fostering echo chambers and amplifying partisan rhetoric, creating the illusion of widespread support that ultimately failed to materialize at the ballot box. This chapter explores how the confluence of celebrity missteps, media bias, and the misuse of social media undermined voter engagement and contributed to a broader crisis of political messaging in the 2024 campaign.

Twitter, TikTok, and Instagram Fed the Illusion of Popularity

Social media platforms like Twitter, TikTok, and Instagram have profoundly reshaped the political landscape, providing campaigns with unprecedented tools for engaging voters, amplifying messages, and mobilizing supporters. These platforms have become central to modern political strategy, particularly for campaigns looking to appeal to younger, tech-savvy audiences. However, the reliance on social media also comes with significant pitfalls, as these platforms inherently create echo chambers that distort reality, leading campaigns to overestimate their popularity. In the 2024 election, the Democratic Party heavily leaned on these platforms to promote its agenda, amplify celebrity endorsements, and energize younger voters. While these efforts generated substantial online attention, they frequently failed to translate into meaningful voter engagement, particularly among critical demographics like working-class and rural voters.

Twitter emerged as a central hub for political discourse, with its short, viral messages driving rapid content sharing and public engagement. Campaigns and influencers relied heavily on Twitter to circulate hashtags, memes, and soundbites that resonated strongly within progressive circles. However, the platform's algorithm, designed to prioritize content that garners high engagement, often amplified extreme or polarizing views while sidelining more nuanced or moderate discussions. This dynamic created a self-reinforcing echo chamber where users were exposed primarily to content that aligned with their existing beliefs, giving campaigns a misleading sense of their reach and impact (Cohn, 2024; Scherer, 2024). For example, tweets promoting progressive policies like climate action and healthcare reform frequently garnered millions of likes and retweets, creating the illusion of widespread enthusiasm. However, these metrics masked the lack of traction these policies had among undecided voters in battleground states, where concerns about job security and economic stability often took precedence over progressive ideals.

TikTok, known for its predominantly younger and tech-savvy user base, became another cornerstone of digital campaigning. The platform's short-form video format allowed political influencers and activists to create engaging, easily digestible content promoting Democratic candidates and mocking their Republican opponents. Videos featuring high-profile endorsements or progressive slogans often went viral, amassing millions of views. However, TikTok's algorithm, which personalizes content feeds based on user behavior, ensured that this content was primarily circulated within echo chambers of already-engaged voters. Studies have shown that TikTok's content rarely breaks through to users with differing political views, making it an ineffective tool for reaching older, moderate, or swing voters who were more likely to decide the outcome of the election (Vincent, 2024). Despite its popularity among younger audiences, the platform's demographic limitations and algorithmic bias meant that its political impact was largely confined to reinforcing existing support rather than expanding the campaign's voter base.

Instagram, with its emphasis on visual storytelling, played a similarly influential role in shaping the Democratic Party's online presence. The platform was used extensively to highlight high-profile endorsements, share polished infographics, and showcase rally footage. These posts often presented an idealized version of the campaign, emphasizing aesthetics and branding over substantive messaging. While Instagram's urban, affluent user base aligned well with certain segments of the Democratic coalition, its reach was limited in rural and working-class communities, where voters were less likely to engage with the platform (Jones, 2024). Additionally, the focus on visually appealing content sometimes reinforced criticisms that the Democratic campaign was more concerned with optics than with addressing real issues. For example, Instagram posts showcasing celebrity endorsements or glamorous campaign events often failed to resonate with voters in economically distressed areas, who viewed such content as emblematic of a campaign disconnected from their struggles.

These platforms, while powerful tools for engagement, contributed to a distorted perception of voter enthusiasm. The viral nature of social media content created a feedback loop, where campaigns mistook online popularity for broad-based support. In reality, the Democratic Party's reliance on Twitter, TikTok, and Instagram often limited its ability to connect with key voter groups outside of its existing base. The platforms' algorithms, designed to maximize engagement rather than foster balanced discourse, exacerbated this problem by creating silos that reinforced ideological divides. As a result, social media buzz often failed to translate into real-world momentum, particularly in battleground states where voter turnout and cross-demographic appeal were critical.

The Democratic Party's experience in 2024 serves as a cautionary tale about the limitations of relying too heavily on social media to gauge voter sentiment. While platforms like Twitter, TikTok, and Instagram can amplify messages and energize specific voter groups, they are not a substitute for comprehensive outreach efforts that engage diverse communities and address their unique concerns. To avoid the illusion of popularity created by social media echo chambers, campaigns must invest in strategies that prioritize substance, inclusivity, and direct voter engagement.

False Assumption That Social Media Buzz Equates to Voter Enthusiasm

One of the most significant missteps of the 2024 election was the Democratic Party's reliance on social media metrics as a proxy for genuine voter enthusiasm. Viral posts, trending hashtags, and large follower counts created an illusion of a groundswell of support, but these metrics failed to reflect the realities of voter turnout and engagement, which ultimately determine electoral outcomes. The weaponization of social media to amplify the Democratic platform not only proved ineffective but also backfired, leaving key voter blocs feeling ignored or alienated.

Social media platforms like TikTok, Instagram, and Twitter were at the center of the Democratic Party's strategy to energize its base and attract new supporters. Through viral videos, influencer campaigns, and carefully crafted hashtags, the party sought to dominate the digital conversation and project an image of overwhelming popularity. However, these efforts largely failed to translate into meaningful action, particularly among younger voters. For example, while platforms like TikTok generated significant buzz around progressive policies and Democratic candidates, the online enthusiasm did not translate into high voter turnout. A 2024 Pew Research study revealed that while 74% of Gen Z voters reported engaging with political content online, only 48% actually turned out to vote in the presidential election (Pew Research Center, 2024). This disparity underscores the limitations of relying on social media as a primary tool for mobilizing voters.

The disconnect between social media activity and real-world voter behavior was further exacerbated by the way these platforms were weaponized. Democratic campaigns heavily invested in influencer partnerships and algorithm-driven outreach, often doubling down on the content that performed well online. These strategies created echo chambers, reinforcing pre-existing support among progressive audiences while failing to reach or persuade undecided voters. For example, Twitter campaigns frequently promoted hashtags like #ClimateJustice or #HealthcareForAll, which resonated within liberal circles but failed to engage working-class or rural voters concerned about job security and economic stability (Cohn, 2024; Scherer, 2024). In essence, the campaigns were preaching to the choir, mistaking viral success for broad appeal.

Additionally, the weaponization of social media amplified the party's reliance on celebrity endorsements, which were heavily promoted across platforms. Posts from celebrity figures garnered millions of likes and shares, creating the impression of widespread influence. However, these endorsements often failed to resonate with voters outside the

Democratic Party's urban and progressive base. Rural and working-class voters, in particular, viewed the focus on celebrity-driven messaging as they are living in a bubble and have no idea as to the true economic and cultural concerns of most Americans. The overemphasis on celebrities further alienated key demographics, reinforcing the perception that the party was more interested in optics than substantive policy solutions (Vincent, 2024). This miscalculation created a feedback loop: social media metrics suggested overwhelming support, leading campaigns to prioritize strategies that ultimately alienated critical voter blocs.

The assumption that social media popularity equated to voter enthusiasm also ignored the demographic limitations of these platforms. While platforms like Instagram and TikTok are highly effective at engaging younger, urban audiences, their reach is limited among older and rural voters, who often rely on more traditional forms of communication. Campaigns focused heavily on digital outreach while neglecting grassroots efforts such as door-to-door canvassing, phone banking, and community events. This imbalance left many voters feeling overlooked, particularly in battleground states where personal connections and local outreach are crucial to winning elections (Jones, 2024).

The overreliance on social media also left campaigns vulnerable to manipulation and backlash. While algorithms prioritized content designed to maximize engagement, this often resulted in the amplification of polarizing or extreme rhetoric, further deepening divisions and alienating moderate voters. The perception that the Democratic Party was catering to the most vocal segments of its base, rather than addressing the concerns of a broader electorate, undermined its ability to build the coalitions needed for electoral success.

Moving Beyond the Echo Chamber

To avoid the pitfalls of social media weaponization and the false assumptions it creates, political campaigns must adopt a more balanced and inclusive approach to voter engagement. While social media can be a powerful tool for amplifying messages, it should be viewed as one component of a broader strategy that includes traditional outreach efforts.

First, campaigns must invest in breaking out of social media echo chambers. This involves crafting content that speaks to diverse audiences, addressing concerns that extend beyond the party's core base. For example, instead of focusing exclusively on progressive issues like climate change, campaigns could highlight bipartisan initiatives such as job creation, infrastructure investment, and affordable healthcare, policies that resonate across demographic and political lines.

Second, campaigns must prioritize converting online engagement into real-world action. This includes organizing voter registration drives, educating voters about polling locations, and addressing systemic barriers to voting, such as transportation challenges or restrictive voter ID laws. By focusing on tangible outcomes rather than digital metrics, campaigns can ensure that social media enthusiasm translates into meaningful electoral participation.

Finally, political leaders must recognize the limitations of celebrity endorsements and algorithm-driven outreach. While these strategies can generate visibility, they are not substitutes for authentic, grassroots engagement. Campaigns must prioritize building relationships with voters in diverse communities, particularly those who are less active online. By engaging directly with working-class, rural, and undecided voters, political leaders can demonstrate a genuine commitment to addressing their concerns.

The 2024 election serves as a cautionary tale about the dangers of mistaking social media buzz for voter enthusiasm. By learning from these missteps and adopting a more inclusive, substance-driven approach, political campaigns can move beyond the traps of the digital echo chamber and build the broad coalitions needed to win elections.

The 2024 presidential election starkly demonstrated the perils of over-reliance on social media, celebrity endorsements, and curated digital narratives. While platforms like Twitter, TikTok, and Instagram created a facade of overwhelming support through viral content and influencer campaigns, they failed to bridge the gap between online engagement and tangible voter turnout. The Democratic Party's heavy investment in these strategies left key voter blocs, working-class, rural, and undecided voters, feeling ignored and alienated, reinforcing perceptions of detachment and elitism.

Social media's echo chambers amplified partisan rhetoric and gave campaigns a false sense of momentum, while high-profile endorsements from celebrities often alienated more than they inspired. These efforts highlighted the limitations of star power and algorithm-driven outreach in addressing the everyday struggles of voters grappling with inflation, healthcare costs, and economic insecurity.

Ultimately, the 2024 campaign revealed that digital dominance is no substitute for authentic, grassroots engagement. Winning elections requires connecting with voters across all demographics and political affiliations, crafting messages that resonate with their immediate concerns rather than catering to ideological silos. The lesson is clear: meaningful political change happens not in the curated feeds of social media but in the trust built through direct, inclusive, and substantive voter engagement. By moving beyond the echo chamber and prioritizing real-world connections, campaigns can reclaim the authenticity and relatability needed to truly resonate with the electorate.

Chapter 9

The Overconfidence Problem

The 2024 election exposed a critical flaw in the Democratic Party's strategy: a dangerous overconfidence rooted in flawed polling, misplaced priorities, and a leadership culture steeped in complacency. Party leaders, buoyed by optimistic internal data and past electoral successes, misjudged the shifting political landscape, assuming their coalition of urban progressives, suburban moderates, and minority voters would remain intact. This hubris led to overreliance on social media buzz, celebrity endorsements, and progressive messaging, while neglecting the bread-and-butter concerns of working-class and rural voters. The illusion of inevitability fostered strategic missteps, from underfunded grassroots operations to a lack of urgency in addressing economic anxieties, leaving the party vulnerable in critical battleground states. This chapter examines how the Democratic Party's overconfidence and detachment from on-the-ground realities contributed to its electoral struggles, offering key lessons for rebuilding trust and broadening its appeal.

Internal Party Polling Versus On-the-Ground Realities

One of the most significant factors contributing to the Democratic Party's struggles in the 2024 election was the disparity between internal polling data and on-the-ground realities. Party leaders relied heavily on sophisticated data models and polls that painted an overly optimistic picture of voter support, failing to account for critical regional and demographic nuances. These overly favorable projections not only led to strategic missteps and resource allocation errors but also fostered a false sense of security among party operatives. This reliance on flawed polling left the campaign unprepared for key challenges in battleground states, where the realities of voter sentiment starkly contrasted with the rosy scenarios projected by internal data.

A major issue with these polls was not just their inaccuracy but the way they were designed, which inadvertently, or perhaps intentionally, introduced bias. Many internal polling strategies were constructed to reflect the narrative the party wanted to promote, emphasizing urban and suburban voter enthusiasm while downplaying signs of discontent among rural and working-class demographics. This inherent bias created a feedback loop where party leaders began to believe their own skewed data, reinforcing their preexisting assumptions about voter support. Instead of questioning whether the polls accurately reflected voter sentiment, leadership often used these numbers to validate their strategic decisions, even when they contradicted reports from local organizers on the ground.

For example, internal polling consistently highlighted strong support among urban and suburban voters, buoyed by social media engagement and favorable demographic trends. However, these metrics ignored the growing dissatisfaction among blue-collar voters in the Rust Belt and the erosion of Democratic support in rural communities. In states like Pennsylvania and Wisconsin, internal models projected narrow but consistent leads for Democratic candidates. Yet post-election analysis revealed that these polls underestimated turnout among conservative voters and overestimated enthusiasm among younger progressives, leading to critical losses in key districts (Cohn, 2024; Scherer, 2024).

One contributing factor to the inaccuracy of these polls was the over-reliance on online surveys and digital engagement metrics, which are inherently skewed toward younger, tech-savvy demographics. While these tools are valuable for gauging certain types of voter behavior, they fail to capture the perspectives of older voters, rural communities, and less digitally connected populations. This reliance created an incomplete and distorted picture of voter sentiment, leading to flawed conclusions about the state of the race. For instance, a 2024 study by the Pew Research Center found that while 68% of surveyed Democrats believed their party was effectively addressing economic issues, only 39% of independent or undecided voters shared this view. This discrepancy, a critical blind spot, was largely missed by internal polling, which leaned heavily on data from supportive demographics (Pew Research Center, 2024).

Moreover, the Democratic Party's faith in its data-driven approach led to a dangerous complacency in ground operations. Believing that they had a strong lead, party leaders redirected resources away from battleground states to shore up support in traditionally blue regions. This strategic error left critical battlegrounds like Arizona and Georgia vulnerable to Republican advances. Studies have determined that in Arizona, Democratic organizers reported that a lack of field staff and on-the-ground volunteers hindered their ability to effectively engage undecided voters, contributing to narrow losses in key districts (Larsson, 2021). This miscalculation was exacerbated by the party's reliance on centralized decision-making, where local concerns were often overlooked in favor of strategies dictated by national leadership.

The bias in polling also created an environment where dissenting voices within the party were dismissed. Field organizers and local leaders who raised concerns about waning enthusiasm or shifting voter priorities were often ignored, as their insights clashed with the optimistic narrative promoted by internal polling. This refusal to engage with on-the-ground realities further widened the gap between the party leadership and the electorate, leaving Democratic candidates ill-prepared to address the issues that ultimately shaped the election outcome.

In hindsight, the Democratic Party's overconfidence in its polling was not merely a technical failing but a symptom of a deeper problem: a leadership culture that prioritized narrative control over genuine voter engagement. By designing polls to validate their assumptions and ignoring evidence of dissent, the party blinded itself to the challenges it faced in critical battleground states. This hubris not only led to strategic errors but also undermined the party's ability to adapt to the evolving political landscape, highlighting the urgent need for a more transparent and inclusive approach to voter outreach and data analysis.

The Democratic Party's overconfidence extended beyond polling missteps to a broader culture of complacency and hubris within its leadership. Buoyed by significant electoral victories in 2020 and 2022, many party leaders assumed that the coalition of urban progressives, suburban moderates, and minority voters that had propelled them to power would remain intact through 2024. This assumption fostered a sense of inevitability about their success, leading to strategic miscalculations, resource misallocations, and a lack of urgency in addressing the evolving concerns of voters. Leadership appeared more focused on maintaining the status quo than adapting to the shifting political landscape, which ultimately alienated critical voter blocs.

A glaring example of this complacency was the Democratic Party's messaging strategy, which often prioritized long-term progressive goals over immediate economic concerns. Policies addressing climate change, healthcare reform, and social justice, while essential, dominated the party's platform at the expense of "kitchen table" issues like inflation, housing affordability, and job security. For many working-class and rural voters, this disconnect reinforced the perception that Democratic leaders were out of touch with the daily struggles of ordinary Americans. While voters grappled with rising costs of living, stagnant wages, and economic uncertainty, the party's focus on aspirational policies failed to resonate with those seeking immediate solutions. Local organizers and field staff frequently warned party leadership about these misaligned priorities, yet their concerns were often dismissed as anecdotal or irrelevant to the broader narrative (Wood and Herbst, 2007).

This disconnect was compounded by the party's reliance on high-profile endorsements and celebrity surrogates. Democratic leaders believed that leveraging star power would energize younger voters and generate enthusiasm across social media platforms. Celebrity endorsements from figures like Beyoncé and others were widely promoted as a strategy to amplify the party's message. However, this approach often alienated key demographics, particularly blue-collar workers and rural voters, who viewed the emphasis on celebrity culture as emblematic of a party more concerned with optics than substance. Instead of inspiring unity, these endorsements often reinforced the perception of elitism, deepening the cultural divide between the party's leadership and many of the voters they sought to win over. Overconfidence in the effectiveness of celebrity endorsements further diverted resources from grassroots organizing, widening the gap between the Democratic leadership and the electorate.

Complacency within the Democratic leadership also extended to voter outreach efforts. Believing that their robust digital strategies and social media campaigns were sufficient to mobilize voters, the party deprioritized traditional forms of engagement, such as door-to-door canvassing, phone banking, and town hall meetings. This decision proved particularly damaging in swing states, where personal connections and face-to-face interactions remain critical for persuading undecided voters. For example, in Michigan, a key battleground state, Democratic field offices reported a significant decline in volunteer numbers and in-person outreach compared to 2020. This decline reflected the party's failure to sustain grassroots momentum and contributed to weaker voter engagement in areas where direct contact could have made a decisive difference (Cohn, 2024; Scherer, 2024).

Moreover, the leadership's overconfidence fostered a sense of insularity, where dissenting opinions and warnings were dismissed as outliers. Local organizers and field staff who voiced concerns about diminishing support among working-class and rural voters were often ignored or marginalized. This top-down approach to decision-making, coupled with an uncritical reliance on overly optimistic internal polling, left the party blind to the warning signs of voter dissatisfaction. Instead of adjusting their strategy to address the economic and cultural concerns of key demographics, Democratic leaders doubled down on their existing narrative, confident that their coalition would hold.

The consequences of this overconfidence were stark. While Republican candidates focused on localized messaging and economic issues, the Democratic Party's reliance on national narratives, data-driven strategies, and celebrity endorsements left it vulnerable to unexpected shifts in voter sentiment. In battleground states, Republican campaigns capitalized on the party's failure to address kitchen-table issues, framing themselves as champions of the working class. Post-election analyses revealed that many Democratic leaders were blindsided by their losses, having underestimated the depth of dissatisfaction among working-class and rural voters. Their complacency not only cost them critical districts but also eroded trust among the very demographics they needed to win future elections.

To rebuild trust and relevance, Democratic leadership must confront the cultural and strategic pitfalls of complacency and hubris. A renewed focus on grassroots engagement, authentic connections with voters, and addressing immediate economic concerns is essential for regaining the support of disillusioned demographics. By listening to the voices of local organizers and prioritizing substance over spectacle, the party can begin to bridge the divide between its leadership and the electorate, avoiding the costly mistakes of 2024.

Rebuilding Through Humility and Focus

Addressing the overconfidence problem will require the Democratic Party to fundamentally overhaul its approach to campaigning, strategy, and voter engagement. The 2024 election exposed significant weaknesses in the party's reliance on overly optimistic polling, misleading data, and a disconnect from its so-called constituents. To rebuild trust and credibility, the party must embrace humility, acknowledge its missteps, and refocus on the needs of all Americans.

First, the Democratic Party must adopt a more cautious and comprehensive approach to polling and voter data. The 2024 election made it clear that the party's overreliance on biased internal polling not only misrepresented voter sentiment but also created a dangerous feedback loop, reinforcing leadership's misplaced confidence. Polling methodologies that skew toward urban, tech-savvy, and progressive respondents must be balanced with traditional techniques, such as phone surveys, in-person interviews, and focus groups. These methods are better equipped to capture the perspectives of rural voters, blue-collar workers, and older demographics often excluded from online polling. Accurate, diverse data will provide a clearer picture of voter priorities, enabling the party to allocate resources more effectively and avoid the embarrassment of relying on false metrics that fail to translate into electoral success.

Second, party leaders must prioritize grassroots organizing and community engagement over high-profile endorsements and flashy digital strategies. The party's fixation on social media virality and celebrity surrogates has not only alienated key demographics but also highlighted its detachment from on-the-ground realities. Building genuine relationships with voters through local events, town halls, and direct outreach is essential for bridging the gap between leadership and the electorate. Grassroots efforts demonstrate that the party values direct engagement and is willing to meet voters where they are— particularly in rural and working-class communities that have felt ignored or dismissed in recent election cycles. By investing in field staff, volunteers, and local organizers, the Democratic Party can rebuild its presence in regions where its influence has waned.

Moreover, the Democratic Party must embrace humility in its messaging and overall strategy. The 2024 election revealed a leadership culture steeped in hubris, with unrealistic expectations and an overinflated sense of its appeal to voters. Leaders often acted as though electoral success was inevitable, relying on a coalition they believed was unshakeable. This attitude not only blinded the party to shifting voter sentiment but also humiliated it when reality proved otherwise. Rebuilding credibility will require a clear acknowledgment of past mistakes and a commitment to listening to the concerns of all Americans, regardless of geography, socioeconomic status, or political affiliation. Humility must replace the assumption that voters will align with the party simply because of shared values or past successes.

The party must also confront its tendency to prioritize spectacle over substance. High-profile endorsements, polished social media campaigns, and celebrity-driven messaging have too often taken precedence over addressing real issues. This approach has alienated voters who are more concerned with inflation, job security, and healthcare than with viral hashtags or celebrity advocacy. Moving forward, the Democratic Party must focus on substantive policies that directly address these concerns and communicate them in a way that resonates with voters from all walks of life.

Finally, the party must reevaluate its expectations and approach each election with a renewed sense of urgency and purpose. The 2024 election underscored the dangers of complacency, as party leaders underestimated the depth of dissatisfaction among working-class and rural voters. To avoid repeating this mistake, the Democratic Party must commit to an inclusive and adaptable strategy that prioritizes voter engagement over assumptions of loyalty. This includes engaging with disillusioned voters who feel left behind and demonstrating through actions, not just words, that their voices matter.

Rebuilding the Democratic Party's credibility and electoral prospects will not be easy, but it is possible with a deliberate focus on humility, inclusivity, and substance. By rejecting overconfidence and embracing a renewed commitment to grassroots engagement and accurate data, the party can begin to heal its relationship with voters and chart a path toward sustainable success. Only by recognizing the lessons of 2024 and addressing its failures can the Democratic Party overcome the humiliation of false assumptions and reestablish itself as a party that truly represents the people.

The 2024 election starkly revealed the Democratic Party's overconfidence as a critical vulnerability, rooted in flawed polling, misplaced priorities, and a complacent leadership culture. This hubris blinded party leaders to shifting voter sentiment, particularly among working-class and rural demographics, and led to strategic missteps that undermined their electoral prospects. Overreliance on celebrity endorsements, social media buzz, and progressive messaging created a false sense of security, masking the urgency of addressing immediate economic concerns and alienating key voter groups.

The disconnect between leadership's assumptions and on-the-ground realities manifested in underfunded grassroots operations, misplaced resource allocation, and a failure to resonate with voters outside the party's core urban and progressive base. Instead of recalibrating their strategy to reflect voter priorities, party leaders doubled down on their existing narrative, assuming loyalty from a coalition that had already begun to fracture.

To rebuild and avoid repeating the costly mistakes of 2024, the Democratic Party must shed its overconfidence and embrace a culture of humility, inclusivity, and adaptability. Genuine engagement with all voters, particularly those who feel overlooked, is critical, as is a renewed focus on bread-and-butter issues like job security, inflation, and healthcare. By prioritizing substance over spectacle and listening to grassroots voices, the party can bridge the divide between leadership and the electorate. Only through this deliberate recalibration can the

Democratic Party regain trust, rebuild its coalition, and chart a sustainable path to future success.

Chapter 10

A Fragmented Message

The fundamental weakness within the Democratic Party: its inability to present a unified and coherent message. Straddling the competing demands of moderates and progressives, the party struggled to articulate a vision that resonated with voters across its broad coalition. This fragmentation diluted its appeal, creating confusion about what the party stood for and alienating key demographics. Conflicting narratives on issues like healthcare, climate change, and economic policy not only divided the party internally but also allowed Republican opponents to frame Democrats as divided and ineffective. Moreover, the Democratic Party's inability to address these fractures left it exposed to criticism and ultimately led to a public embarrassment on the national stage. The lack of cohesion, compounded by misaligned priorities and ineffective outreach, undermined its electoral prospects, leaving the party to confront its internal divisions and the significant loss of voter trust. This chapter examines how the Democrats' fragmented messaging and disarray contributed to a humiliating and consequential defeat in 2024.

Conflicting Narratives, Moderate vs Progressive, Diluted the Party's Appeal

One of the most significant challenges facing the Democratic Party in the 2024 election was its inability to present a cohesive and unified message. The party's broad coalition, encompassing moderates, progressives, and independents, has long been both a strength and a weakness. In 2024, this diversity of perspectives resulted in conflicting narratives that diluted the party's appeal and muddied its policy priorities. The ideological tug-of-war between moderates and progressives prevented the Democrats from articulating a clear vision, leaving voters uncertain about what the party truly stood for.

The tension between moderate and progressive wings of the Democratic Party was evident in debates over key policy areas such as healthcare, climate change, and criminal justice reform. Moderates favored incremental reforms aimed at preserving broad appeal, while progressives championed sweeping systemic changes. For example, on healthcare, moderates advocated expanding the Affordable Care Act, while progressives pushed for Medicare for All. This division was reflected in campaign messaging for more than 5 years, where candidates struggled to balance the competing demands of their constituencies (Larsson, 2021). Instead of presenting a unified front, the party often sent mixed signals, alienating both centrist voters who feared radical changes and progressives who felt their priorities were being sidelined.

Social media further exacerbated these divisions, as platforms like Twitter and TikTok amplified the voices of progressive activists who often clashed with moderate party leaders. While these activists generated significant online attention, their influence sometimes overshadowed the broader coalition, giving the impression that the party was more ideologically extreme than it actually was (Cohn, 2024; Scherer, 2024). This perception alienated moderate and independent voters, particularly in swing states where Republicans successfully framed Democrats as out of touch with mainstream America.

The lack of a cohesive narrative also undermined the party's ability to respond effectively to Republican attacks. GOP candidates capitalized on the Democrats' fragmented messaging, portraying them as divided and incapable of governing. In battleground states like Pennsylvania and Arizona, Republican campaigns highlighted the contradictions between moderate and progressive Democratic candidates, using their policy disagreements as evidence of disarray. This strategy resonated with voters who were already skeptical of the party's ability to deliver on its promises (Wood and Herbst, 2007).

The fragmented message also contributed to internal tensions within the Democratic Party. Progressive activists criticized party leadership for prioritizing electability over bold policy proposals, while moderates warned that an overly progressive platform could alienate key voter blocs. These disagreements often played out publicly, creating the perception of a divided party more focused on internal conflicts than on addressing voter concerns. This lack of unity was particularly damaging in an election where the Republicans presented a more disciplined and focused message, emphasizing economic recovery and cultural values that appealed to a broad range of voters.

Challenges of Uniting a Coalition That Spans Generations, Geographies, and Ideologies

The Democratic Party's coalition is one of the most diverse in American politics, encompassing a wide range of generational, geographical, and ideological perspectives. While this diversity is a source of strength, it also presents significant challenges in building a cohesive and united platform. The 2024 election underscored the difficulty of addressing the varied priorities of such a broad coalition while maintaining a consistent and compelling message.

Generational divides within the Democratic Party posed one of the most significant challenges. Younger voters, particularly Millennials and Gen Z, tend to prioritize progressive issues such as climate action, racial justice, and student loan forgiveness. In contrast, older

Democrats often focus on more traditional concerns like Social Security, Medicare, and national security (Pew Research Center, 2024). These differences in priorities made it difficult for the party to craft a platform that resonated across age groups. For example, while younger voters supported aggressive climate policies, older voters expressed concerns about the economic impact of transitioning away from fossil fuels. This generational divide was further complicated by differences in communication styles, with younger voters favoring digital engagement and older voters preferring more traditional forms of outreach.

Geographical divides added another layer of complexity. Urban voters, who form a significant portion of the Democratic base, often prioritize issues like public transportation, housing affordability, and police reform. In contrast, rural voters, many of whom are skeptical of the party's progressive agenda, are more concerned with agricultural policy, access to healthcare, and economic development (Wood and Herbst, 2007). Reconciling these differing priorities proved challenging, particularly in battleground states where Democrats needed to appeal to both urban and rural constituencies.

Ideological divides within the party further complicated efforts to build a cohesive coalition. While progressives called for bold systemic changes, moderates emphasized pragmatism and incremental reforms. These ideological differences often played out in high-profile policy debates, such as the push for Medicare for All versus expanding the Affordable Care Act. The party's inability to reconcile these competing visions left voters uncertain about what Democrats stood for and whether they could deliver on their promises.

The Democratic Party's challenges in uniting its coalition were compounded by its reliance on top-down messaging strategies that often failed to reflect the concerns of local communities. In swing states like Michigan and Wisconsin, voters expressed frustration that national messaging did not address their specific needs, such as manufacturing job losses and infrastructure decay. This disconnect highlighted the limitations of a one-size-fits-all approach to campaigning and underscored the need for a more localized and inclusive strategy.

To overcome these challenges, the Democratic Party must adopt a more collaborative approach to policymaking and messaging. This includes fostering dialogue between different factions within the party, ensuring that all voices are heard and represented in the platform. By prioritizing shared values and emphasizing common goals, the party can build a more cohesive narrative that resonates across its diverse coalition. Additionally, Democrats must invest in grassroots organizing and community engagement to better understand and address the unique needs of different voter groups. Only by bridging its internal divides can the party present a united front and regain the trust of the electorate.

Chapter 11

The Republican Playbook

The 2024 election showcased a Republican Party revitalized by strategic discipline, targeted messaging, and an ability to capitalize on Democratic missteps. By focusing on kitchen-table issues such as inflation, job creation, and public safety, Republicans effectively framed themselves as champions of everyday Americans while portraying Democrats as out-of-touch elites. Their unified narrative and commitment to grassroots engagement contrasted sharply with the fragmented messaging and overreliance on celebrity endorsements that plagued their opponents. Beyond consolidating their traditional base, Republicans made significant inroads into traditionally Democratic territories, successfully appealing to working-class voters, socially conservative minorities, and suburban swing voters. This chapter explores how the Republican Party not only seized the moment to highlight Democratic failures but also strategically expanded its reach, cementing its position as a dominant force in American politics.

Breakdown of the Republican Strategy That Capitalized on Democratic Missteps

The Republican Party's success in the 2024 election can be largely attributed to its ability to craft a disciplined, focused strategy that exploited the Democratic Party's missteps and resonated with a broad swath of the electorate. Unlike their opponents, Republicans avoided the pitfalls of fragmented messaging and disconnection from key voter blocs, presenting themselves as a stable and pragmatic alternative. By refining in on voter concerns and addressing them with clear, actionable policies, the GOP effectively tapped into widespread frustration over economic instability, cultural tensions, and a perceived lack of leadership from Democrats. This ability to identify and capitalize on weaknesses in the Democratic campaign, such as overreliance on social media, reliance on celebrity endorsements, and neglect of rural and working-class communities, proved decisive in their success.

At the core of the Republican playbook was a relentless focus on "kitchen table issues" that directly impacted voters' daily lives. Inflation, job creation, energy independence, and public safety were central themes across Republican campaigns. In contrast to the Democrats' focus on long-term progressive goals like combating climate change and overhauling healthcare, Republican candidates prioritized immediate concerns. In battleground states like Pennsylvania and Wisconsin, they framed themselves as defenders of the working class, contrasting their approach with Democratic policies they argued would harm key industries like manufacturing and fossil fuels. By emphasizing these issues, Republicans built a narrative that resonated strongly with voters who felt neglected or actively harmed by Democratic priorities (Larsson, 2021). This strategic positioning allowed Republicans to build trust among voters who saw them as advocates for economic stability and cultural preservation.

Republicans further capitalized on the Democrats' reliance on celebrity endorsements and social media-driven strategies, portraying these tactics as emblematic of a party disconnected from ordinary Americans. While the Democrats amplified celebrity surrogates and polished media campaigns, Republicans grounded their efforts in grassroots engagement. GOP candidates frequently appeared in traditional settings, such as town halls, community events, and local businesses, where they interacted directly with constituents. These appearances fostered a sense of authenticity and relatability, highlighting the Republicans' understanding of everyday struggles (Brownstein, 2024; Neubarth, 2024; Tanenhaus, 2025). The contrast was stark: while Democrats generated viral social media moments, Republicans cultivated real-world connections that translated into voter trust and turnout. This strategic choice not only counteracted the Democrats' dominance in digital media but also reinforced the Republican narrative of being the party of the people.

Another critical component of the Republican strategy was their disciplined messaging. In stark contrast to the Democrats, whose internal divisions led to conflicting narratives, the Republican Party presented a unified front. Across campaigns nationwide, Republican candidates consistently echoed core themes: economic stability, cultural preservation, and opposition to what they labeled as "woke" policies. This consistency solidified their base while also appealing to independents and moderate Democrats disillusioned with the progressive agenda. For instance, Republicans framed their opposition to progressive climate policies as a defense of jobs in traditional industries, positioning themselves as protectors of economic opportunity. This cohesive messaging avoided the pitfalls of fragmentation that hampered Democratic efforts and allowed Republicans to build a broader coalition of support.

Republicans also successfully blended modern and traditional campaign tactics, leveraging targeted advertising and data-driven outreach alongside grassroots organizing. While they invested heavily in digital marketing to reach younger and suburban voters, they balanced this with traditional voter contact methods, such as phone banking, door-to-door canvassing, and direct mail. This multifaceted approach proved particularly effective in battleground states, where campaigns tailored their messaging to address specific local concerns. For example, in Arizona, Republican candidates emphasized immigration and border security, issues of particular importance to voters in the region. In Michigan, the focus was on revitalizing manufacturing and investing in infrastructure, themes that resonated deeply with working-class voters (Wood and Herbst, 2007). These localized strategies ensured that Republican messaging was relevant and impactful, reinforcing their connection with voters.

The Republican Party's disciplined strategy in 2024 showcased the effectiveness of clear, consistent messaging and grassroots engagement. By prioritizing kitchen table issues, presenting a unified front, and tailoring their campaigns to address regional concerns, Republicans not only capitalized on Democratic missteps but also positioned themselves as the party of pragmatism and responsiveness. Their ability to connect with voters on both an emotional and practical level solidified their resurgence and offered a blueprint for future electoral success.

How They Rebuilt Their Own Base and Expanded into Traditionally Democratic Territories

In addition to capitalizing on Democratic weaknesses, the Republican Party made significant strides in rebuilding its base and expanding into territories traditionally considered Democratic strongholds. This resurgence was driven by a targeted approach that re-engaged disillusioned voters, attracted new demographics, and fostered long-term loyalty through grassroots organizing and locally tailored policies.

A key component of the Republican resurgence was their ability to reconnect with working-class voters, particularly in the Rust Belt. By emphasizing economic policies that prioritized job creation, trade protectionism, and energy independence, Republicans effectively appealed to voters who had felt neglected by the Democratic Party's focus on progressive social policies. In states like Ohio, Pennsylvania, and Wisconsin, Republican candidates framed themselves as defenders of traditional industries such as manufacturing and coal, leveraging frustration over job losses and economic stagnation. By advocating for policies that resonated with blue-collar workers, the GOP reinforced their image as the party that understood and supported working-class America (Brownstein, 2024; Neubarth, 2024; Tanenhaus, 2025). This strategy was particularly effective in regions where industries had been hollowed out by globalization and automation and where promises of economic revival struck a deep chord with voters.

The Republican Party also made notable inroads with Hispanic and African American voters, particularly in states like Florida and Texas, where culturally conservative values play a significant role in shaping political preferences. Republicans focused on issues such as religious freedom, parental rights in education, and opposition to progressive education policies. These messages resonated strongly with socially conservative minorities who had traditionally aligned with the Democratic Party. For example, the GOP's support for school choice and critique of progressive curricula were especially popular among Hispanic voters, who increasingly viewed the Republican Party as more aligned with their family-centered values and concerns about educational opportunities for their children (Larsson, 2021). This outreach helped the GOP chip away at long-standing Democratic majorities in diverse communities, reshaping the electoral map in key states.

In rural areas, Republicans deepened their influence by addressing specific concerns related to agricultural policy, land use, and access to healthcare. Unlike Democrats, who often focused on urban-centric issues, Republicans crafted platforms that directly addressed the needs of rural communities. Proposals to expand broadband access, protect agricultural subsidies, and improve rural healthcare infrastructure appealed to voters who felt overlooked by the Democratic Party. This strategy not only solidified the Republican base in rural regions but also attracted moderate voters seeking practical solutions to their unique challenges.

In traditionally Democratic urban and suburban areas, Republicans strategically targeted moderate and independent voters who were dissatisfied with rising crime rates, inflation, and housing costs. By positioning themselves as champions of public safety and economic stability, Republican candidates successfully swayed voters who believed the Democratic Party had failed to address these pressing issues. For example, in suburban districts outside Philadelphia, GOP candidates focused on crime reduction, property tax relief, and educational reform. These targeted efforts resonated with swing voters who had previously leaned Democratic but were increasingly frustrated with the perceived inability of Democratic leaders to manage local and national crises effectively (Wood and Herbst, 2007).

The Republican Party's ability to rebuild and expand its base was further strengthened by its emphasis on grassroots organizing. Unlike the Democrats, who often relied on top-down strategies dictated by national leadership, Republicans empowered state and county organizations to tailor their efforts to the unique needs of their communities. This decentralized approach allowed the GOP to build trust and establish long-term relationships with voters, fostering loyalty that extended beyond individual election cycles. Grassroots organizing efforts included door-to-door canvassing, town hall meetings, and direct voter outreach, which reinforced the party's connection to local concerns and bolstered turnout in critical districts.

The combination of targeted policies, localized outreach, and grassroots engagement enabled the Republican Party to rebuild and expand its base in ways that fundamentally reshaped the political landscape. By addressing the needs of diverse communities and emphasizing shared values, Republicans not only consolidated their traditional support but also made inroads into key demographics and regions that had long been considered Democratic strongholds. This multifaceted strategy provided the foundation for their 2024 success and positioned the party for sustained influence in future elections.

Chapter 12

Election Night 2024

The air was electric with anticipation as Americans tuned in to watch the culmination of one of the most contentious and polarizing presidential campaigns in recent history. For the Democratic Party, the night began with optimism, buoyed by weeks of polling that predicted Kamala Harris would secure a historic victory as the first Black woman president. Campaign headquarters were abuzz with activity, with staff and supporters preparing to celebrate what they believed was a foregone conclusion. However, as the results trickled in, a sense of disbelief began to settle over the room. Counties thought to be safely Democratic turned unexpectedly red, while turnout in key urban centers failed to meet expectations. By the time the clock struck midnight, the unthinkable had happened: battleground states like Pennsylvania, Wisconsin, and Arizona had swung decisively Republican, shattering the Democratic coalition and delivering a stunning defeat. The disbelief, the fallout, and the lessons of that night would shape the political landscape for years to come.

A Night of Disbelief and Fallout

Election night in 2024 will be remembered as a seismic shift in the political landscape, a night that shattered Democratic hopes and sent shockwaves through their coalition. The Democratic Party, buoyed by glowing internal polling and the belief that Kamala Harris's historic candidacy would galvanize a diverse electorate, approached the evening with confidence. High-profile endorsements, aggressive digital campaigns, and months of meticulous strategy seemed to have secured what many believed was a clear path to victory. Yet as the results began to unfold, that confidence eroded into disbelief and despair.

The evening started with cautious optimism. In the early hours after the polls closed on the East Coast, results trickled in from Democratic strongholds like New York and Massachusetts, providing the expected wins. Yet even in these traditionally safe areas, turnout was not as robust as predicted, particularly among younger voters who had been a key focus of the Harris campaign. As returns from critical swing states like Pennsylvania, Wisconsin, and Arizona began to roll in, the mood at Harris's campaign headquarters in Washington, D.C., turned from celebratory to tense. Despite months of polling suggesting narrow but consistent Democratic leads in these battlegrounds, early returns painted a starkly different picture.

By 9:00 PM Eastern Time, it was becoming clear that the Republican nominee had mobilized a powerful coalition of rural, suburban, and working-class voters. Counties thought to be safely Democratic were posting narrower margins than expected, while Republican strongholds reported record turnout. Tensions rose as campaign aides huddled around screens, poring over data and seeking paths to victory in an increasingly grim electoral map. States like Michigan and Wisconsin, long considered Democratic strongholds, were slipping out of reach.

The tipping point came shortly after midnight when news networks began projecting a Republican win in Pennsylvania, a state widely regarded as a cornerstone of Democratic strategy. By this point, projections for Arizona and Wisconsin had also turned red, sealing the Republican nominee's victory. As the gravity of the loss became undeniable, campaign staff scrambled to craft a concession speech. Kamala Harris emerged at 2:30 AM, delivering a somber yet resilient address. Acknowledging the devastating defeat, she emphasized the need for unity and continued progress, even as her supporters watched with disbelief.

Key States and Demographics That Swung the Election

1. Pennsylvania: The Keystone State's Shift

The loss of Pennsylvania was a devastating blow to the Democratic campaign, which had heavily relied on strong urban turnout in cities like Philadelphia and Pittsburgh. While these areas delivered Democratic majorities, the margins were far smaller than anticipated. Turnout among young and minority voters, groups the Harris campaign had aggressively targeted, fell short of expectations. Meanwhile, Republican messaging resonated strongly in rural and suburban areas, particularly among coal and manufacturing workers.

Economic concerns dominated the discourse in Pennsylvania, with 58% of voters citing the economy as their top issue, according to exit polls (Pew Research Center, 2024). Republican promises of energy independence and job creation struck a chord, especially in coal-producing regions where Democratic environmental policies were perceived as threatening livelihoods. By the time all votes were counted, the Republican nominee had flipped key counties in northeastern Pennsylvania, securing a narrow but decisive victory.

2. Wisconsin: The Fall of a Democratic Stronghold

Wisconsin, once a reliable part of the Democratic "Blue Wall," delivered another crushing loss. Rural voters turned out in record numbers, energized by Republican messaging that championed traditional industries and cultural conservatism. Dairy farmers and agricultural communities, long frustrated by what they viewed as Democratic elitism, overwhelmingly backed the Republican nominee.

Exit polls showed that 62% of Wisconsin voters felt the Democratic Party was out of touch with rural America (Cohn, 2024; Scherer, 2024). Meanwhile, suburban counties, particularly those surrounding Milwaukee, showed signs of wavering. Concerns about rising crime, economic uncertainty, and education policy drove many moderate suburban voters to shift toward the Republican camp. While Democratic turnout remained strong in urban centers like Madison and Milwaukee, it was not enough to offset the Republican gains in rural and suburban areas.

3. Arizona: A Rising Star for the GOP

Arizona, a state Democrats had hoped to secure, emerged as a battleground where the Republican Party made significant inroads. The Harris campaign had focused on progressive social policies, including immigration reform and climate action, but these priorities failed to resonate with many voters in the state.

Latino voters, a key demographic in Arizona, played a critical role in the outcome. While Democrats had traditionally relied on strong Latino support, exit polls revealed a growing dissatisfaction with the party's perceived inaction on economic and border security issues. In a prior survey, sixty-four percent of Latino voters in Arizona ranked economic stability as their top concern, with many expressing frustration over inflation and job insecurity (Larsson, 2021). High turnout in Maricopa County, driven by Republican gains in suburban areas, ultimately tipped the state in the GOP's favor.

4. The Demographics That Broke the Coalition

- **Rural Voters:** Rural Americans delivered a decisive blow to the Democratic campaign. Republican messaging framed the Democratic platform as dismissive of small-town values and agricultural industries, resonating with rural voters who felt overlooked. Nationwide, rural voters accounted for 67% of the Republican vote, highlighting a growing cultural and economic divide (Gallup, 2024).

- **Working-Class Voters:** Once a cornerstone of the Democratic coalition, working-class voters turned out in droves for the Republican nominee. Exit polls showed that 62% of voters without a college degree favored Republican policies, citing concerns about inflation, stagnant wages, and job security (Pew Research Center, 2024).

- **Suburban Voters:** Suburban areas, long a battleground, shifted toward the Republican Party. Rising concerns about crime, education policy, and economic stability drove moderate suburban voters to reconsider their allegiance. This reversion was particularly pronounced in key swing states like Pennsylvania and Arizona.

Fallout of Failed Expectations of the 2024 Presidential Election

The fallout from election night was swift and severe, with Democratic leaders facing a torrent of criticism for their overconfidence, strategic missteps, and failure to address the pressing concerns of working-class and rural voters. The Democratic Party's reliance on social media metrics, celebrity endorsements, and progressive messaging, which resonated strongly in urban and coastal strongholds, proved alienating to the majority of the electorate. Pundits lambasted the party for focusing on long-term ideals at the expense of immediate economic concerns, while grassroots organizers pointed to a lack of direct engagement with key communities. Divisions erupted within party ranks, as insiders and leaders scrambled to assign blame for the resounding defeat.

The Republican victory was nothing short of historic. By successfully appealing to a broad coalition of rural, suburban, and working-class voters, the Republican candidate swept not only the White House but also secured decisive majorities in both the House of Representatives and the Senate. This trifecta of political control granted the party unprecedented power to set the legislative agenda and roll back Democratic policies. Even more telling, the Republican nominee won the popular vote, signaling a nationwide repudiation of the Democratic Party's perceived detachment from the frustrations of average Americans.

Voter turnout across the board revealed the depths of this discontent. Key demographics, once considered stalwart Democratic constituencies, shifted their allegiances. Blue-collar voters, disillusioned by stagnant wages and rising living costs, gravitated toward Republican promises of economic revitalization. Suburban moderates, concerned about inflation, education, and safety, abandoned the Democrats in favor of a party they saw as better addressing their daily realities. Rural voters, feeling long ignored, turned out in record numbers, delivering decisive margins in critical battleground states.

The scope of the Republican victory underscored just how profoundly the Democrats had miscalculated the national mood. Polls and campaign strategies failed to account for widespread frustration with Washington's gridlock, a sentiment Republicans adeptly capitalized on by presenting themselves as agents of change. The election results served as a sharp rebuke not only to the Democratic Party's policy priorities but also to its campaign apparatus, which increasingly disconnected from reality with the electorate's immediate needs.

Election night 2024 was more than a defeat for the Democratic Party, it was a reckoning. The loss exposed glaring weaknesses in their coalition and highlighted the dangers of assuming loyalty from core constituencies without addressing their concerns. For the Republicans, the victory marked a resounding validation of their focus on economic and cultural issues, solidifying their mandate to govern. For the Democrats, it ignited a period of introspection, forcing leaders to confront the failures that led to such a comprehensive and humbling defeat. The lessons of that night would reverberate for years, reshaping both party platforms and the broader trajectory of American politics.

Finally, the 2024 election delivered a sharp and painful blow to the Democratic Party, shattering their confidence and exposing the fragility of their coalition. What was anticipated as a historic triumph for Kamala Harris instead became a sobering reckoning with the realities of an electorate increasingly disillusioned with progressive platitudes and political complacency. The sweeping Republican victory, capturing the presidency, both houses of Congress, and even the popular vote, underscored the depth of frustration among voters who felt ignored and marginalized. For the Democrats, this was not just a loss of power, it was a loss of connection to the very people they claimed to champion. The sting of defeat was magnified by their own miscalculations, as overconfidence, strategic missteps, and an inability to adapt to the shifting political landscape left them unprepared for the wave of discontent that swept the nation. The lessons of 2024 are stark and unforgiving: to rebuild, the Democratic Party must abandon its reliance on hollow optics and rediscover the art of listening, understanding, and delivering for a diverse and increasingly skeptical electorate.

Chapter 13

The Post-Mortem

The aftermath of the 2024 election was marked by a wave of introspection, blame-shifting, and public critique as Democrats and political analysts sought to unravel the causes of a defeat that few had anticipated. Immediate reactions from party insiders ranged from defensive justifications to outright denunciations of campaign strategy, while voters and pundits offered scathing assessments of a campaign that seemed increasingly out of touch with the national mood. Compounding the fallout was the role of media outlets, many of which had missed or actively spun the story, creating an echo chamber that shielded the Democratic Party from the warning signs of voter discontent. The post-mortem of the 2024 election offered stark lessons about the perils of overconfidence, the limitations of elite narratives, and the widening gap between political leadership and the electorate.

A Campaign Caught Off Guard

The shock of the 2024 defeat reverberated across Democratic leadership as the magnitude of the loss became clear. What had been framed as a night to celebrate Kamala Harris's historic ascension to the presidency quickly unraveled into a frenzy of blame-shifting, self-reflection, and political fallout. The decision to replace President Joe Biden with Harris on the ticket, a move intended to invigorate the base and address growing concerns about Biden's age and leadership, now stood as a lightning rod for criticism. The gambit, orchestrated by top party figures including Nancy Pelosi and Senate Majority Leader Chuck Schumer, was viewed in hindsight as a disastrous miscalculation that ignored the pulse of constituents.

Within days of the election, Washington, D.C., became the epicenter of Democratic introspection. Closed-door meetings among party insiders revealed deep fissures in the party's strategy, with campaign operatives accusing polling teams of providing overly optimistic projections and field organizers lambasting leadership for dismissing their warnings about voter sentiment. The fractures highlighted the party's inability to unite its progressive and centrist factions, a failure that many believed played a pivotal role in their electoral collapse.

Prominent Democratic figures were quick to air their grievances publicly. Senator Elizabeth Warren expressed frustration over the party's disconnect from working-class voters, tweeting, "We lost because we didn't listen. Economic security is the foundation of every family's future, jobs, housing, and healthcare need to be our focus" (@ewarren, 2024). Meanwhile, Nancy Pelosi, who had played a key role in the decision to transition Biden out of the race, defended the move in a *CNN* interview but acknowledged the party's strategic failures. "We believed Kamala Harris could unite the coalition and energize key demographics. Clearly, we underestimated the frustration of many Americans who felt left behind," Pelosi admitted (CNN, 2024).

Centrist Democrats, led by Senator Joe Manchin and Representative Abigail Spanberger, openly criticized the party's progressive wing for dominating the narrative at the expense of practical solutions. "We spent too much time focusing on issues that divide and not enough on the kitchen-table concerns that unite," Manchin told *The Hill*. "People care about affordability, job security, and safety. That's where we lost them" (Pew, 2024). Spanberger echoed these sentiments in an op-ed for *The Washington Post*, warning that the party's focus on progressive social policies alienated suburban moderates and rural voters who felt abandoned by national leadership (Kessler, 2024).

The Fallout of Replacing Biden

The decision to replace Joe Biden as the Democratic nominee was intended to project vitality and progressiveness, but it backfired spectacularly. Biden, already facing declining approval ratings, had been seen by party leaders as a liability in a general election. Persistent Republican attack ads highlighting his age and verbal gaffes further fueled concerns about his viability. Under mounting pressure from Democratic insiders, Biden reluctantly stepped aside in mid-2023, paving the way for Harris to become the presumptive nominee.

At the time, the move was heralded by leaders like Pelosi and Schumer as a necessary step to secure electoral success. Harris's candidacy was seen as historic, and her appeal to younger voters, women, and minorities was expected to reinvigorate the Democratic base. However, the lack of a primary process, intended to avoid internal divisions, sparked resentment among grassroots activists and alienated moderate voters who felt excluded from the decision-making process. Critics argued that the transition came across as undemocratic and elitist, further amplifying the party's image problem.

This perception only deepened as the campaign unfolded. While Harris's team leaned heavily on progressive messaging and celebrity endorsements, they failed to address mounting economic anxieties. Exit polls revealed that 68% of voters prioritized inflation and job security over social and environmental policies, with many swing voters viewing the Democratic platform as disconnected from their daily struggles (Pew Research Center, 2024). Harris's inability to articulate clear solutions to these concerns only reinforced the narrative that the Democratic Party is disconnected from Americans reality.

Grassroots Frustration and Public Backlash

Grassroots organizers expressed palpable frustration with party leadership, accusing them of ignoring early warnings about voter discontent. A field organizer from Pennsylvania, interviewed by *Politico*, recounted multiple attempts to alert the national campaign about economic concerns dominating conversations with voters. "We were talking about inflation and job losses, but the party was talking about climate justice and celebrity endorsements. It was like we were living in two different worlds" (Smith, 2024).

I felt that same disconnect during my time in both industry and higher education. There were days I left meetings wondering, "Do they even care about the people we're here to serve?" Politics had become a performance, and I was exhausted from playing a role I never auditioned for.

Voters echoed this sentiment, with many expressing a sense of betrayal. In interviews conducted by the Pew Research Center, former Democratic supporters cited rising living costs, stagnant wages, and housing affordability as their primary concerns, issues they felt were ignored by Harris's campaign. Sixty-two percent of swing voters described the Democratic Party as "out of touch," while 58% agreed that the party prioritized progressive ideals over pragmatic solutions (Pew Research Center, 2024).

Social media, which had been a cornerstone of the Democratic campaign, became a battleground of disillusionment. Platforms like Twitter and Facebook were flooded with posts criticizing the party's reliance on celebrities and viral campaigns. Many posts highlighted the stark contrast between polished digital messaging and the lived realities of working- and middle-class Americans

Media's Role: Missing the Story

The media's role in the 2024 election added another layer of complexity to the Democratic Party's defeat, revealing not just a failure to capture the electorate's pulse but also an overt weaponization of coverage to steer the narrative in favor of Kamala Harris. Mainstream outlets like *The New York Times*, *CNN*, *MSNBC*, and *The Washington Post* largely celebrated Harris's candidacy, often highlighting its historic nature and cultural significance while glossing over pressing voter concerns such as inflation, housing, and healthcare. High-profile anchors such as Don Lemon, Joy Reid, and Anderson Cooper routinely offered personal opinions about Harris's leadership qualities as if they were incontrovertible facts, creating a perception among voters—especially those outside Democratic strongholds—that the media was functioning less as a neutral observer and more as an active participant in the campaign.

On MSNBC, Rachel Maddow dedicated an entire segment to discussing Harris's "inspirational rise" and referred to her as "a unifying force in American politics," framing this assertion as an undisputed reality rather than an analysis (National Review, 2024; Noonan, 2024). Similarly, on *CNN*, anchor Jake Tapper praised Harris during a panel discussion, stating, "Kamala Harris's vision for America represents the future we should all aspire to," a statement that blurred the lines between reporting and personal advocacy (CNN, 2024). These moments of uncritical celebration, while effective at energizing progressive audiences, alienated moderates and conservatives who viewed the coverage as overtly partisan and disconnected from the concerns of everyday Americans.

When the News Becomes the Narrative

Critics argued that the media created an echo chamber that insulated the Democratic Party from inconvenient truths about the electorate's priorities. A report by the *Media Research Center* revealed that 72% of election coverage on major networks emphasized progressive social justice themes, while only 15% addressed economic concerns like inflation, job creation, and housing (MRC, 2024). This imbalance mirrored and amplified the Democratic Party's strategic blind spots, as the narratives pushed by media outlets failed to resonate with working-class and rural voters struggling with rising costs and economic instability.

For example, Joy Reid on *MSNBC* referred to the Republican campaign as "a fear-driven strategy" that capitalized on "unfounded grievances" among working-class Americans (National Review, 2024; Noonan, 2024). While her analysis aligned with progressive perspectives, it dismissed the genuine economic anxieties driving voter behavior in key battleground states. This kind of dismissive rhetoric not only alienated voters but also contributed to a broader perception that liberal media outlets is completely disconnected from the reality of middle-class and rural communities.

A Stark Disparity in Media Treatment

The stark contrast in media treatment of Kamala Harris and Donald Trump became one of the most glaring controversies of the election. Harris was frequently portrayed as an inspiring trailblazer, with interviews framed as opportunities to showcase her achievements, personal story, and vision for the future. For instance, on *CNN's* town hall, Anderson Cooper opened by asking Harris about her personal heroes and how her presidency would "bring hope to a divided nation," framing the interview as a celebration of her candidacy rather than a critical examination.

In contrast, Trump's interviews were characterized by relentless scrutiny and adversarial questioning. During an interview on *NBC's Meet the Press*, host Kristen Welker opened with, "Mr. Trump, how do you defend your record amidst ongoing investigations and accusations of divisiveness?" While tough questioning is an essential aspect of journalism, the disparity in tone and content was stark. Trump frequently faced detailed inquiries into his legal battles, rhetoric, and controversial policies, while Harris's interviews often avoided similarly challenging topics.

116

Fact-checking segments further underscored this imbalance. Outlets like *The Washington Post* devoted extensive resources to dissecting Trump's statements, labeling them as "misleading" or "false," while providing comparatively lenient analysis of Harris's claims. For instance, a *Washington Post* fact-check on Harris's healthcare policy framed her proposals as "ambitious but achievable" despite criticism from economists about their potential costs (Kessler, 2024). This discrepancy fueled accusations from conservative commentators that the media was actively working to protect Harris from scrutiny while magnifying Trump's flaws.

Weaponizing Media Narratives

The weaponization of media narratives extended beyond interviews and fact-checking to broader coverage strategies. Headlines in *The New York Times* and *The Washington Post* frequently lauded Harris's campaign milestones, with phrases like "Kamala Harris's transformative leadership" and "Harris as the face of progress in America." Meanwhile, Trump was consistently portrayed in negative terms, with headlines focusing on his "legal woes," "divisive rhetoric," and "polarizing policies."

This disparity in narrative framing did not go unnoticed by voters. A survey conducted by the Pew Research Center found that 64% of Americans believed the media displayed overt bias in its election coverage, with 75% of conservative respondents and 58% of independents agreeing that the mainstream media favored the Democratic Party (Pew Research Center, 2024). Conservative outlets like *Fox News* and *The Wall Street Journal* seized on this perception, framing the election as not just a battle between political ideologies but also a referendum on media fairness.

Social media platforms like Twitter, TikTok, and Instagram compounded these dynamics by amplifying partisan content. Trending hashtags like #MadamPresident and #Harris2024 dominated online discourse, creating an illusion of widespread support for Harris's campaign. Algorithms prioritized content that generated high engagement, often at the expense of balanced or nuanced perspectives. David Frum, writing for *The Atlantic*, noted, "Social media didn't just distort reality for voters—it distorted it for Democratic leaders, who mistook digital applause for genuine voter enthusiasm" (Frum, 2024).

The media's role in the 2024 election was pivotal but deeply polarizing. By blending opinion with reporting and amplifying partisan narratives, outlets like *CNN*, *MSNBC*, and *The New York Times* shaped a campaign environment that both energized progressive voters and alienated moderates and conservatives. The disparity in treatment between Kamala Harris and Donald Trump further reinforced perceptions of bias, undermining trust in journalistic impartiality. In the end, the media's weaponization of its voice not only failed to deliver the anticipated Democratic victory but also deepened divisions within the electorate, leaving a lasting impact on public trust in the press.

Social Media: Distorting Reality

The media's role in shaping the 2024 election narrative was amplified by social media platforms like Twitter, Instagram, and TikTok, which became key battlegrounds for public opinion. These platforms, driven by engagement-focused algorithms, prioritized sensational and polarizing content, creating an echo chamber that amplified Democratic messaging while marginalizing other perspectives. Viral hashtags such as #MadamPresident and #Kamala2024 dominated the digital discourse, flooding feeds with celebratory posts, inspirational soundbites, and endorsements from celebrities and influencers. This carefully curated digital landscape gave the impression of an unstoppable Democratic juggernaut, fostering a sense of inevitability around Harris's campaign.

However, the viral energy on these platforms failed to translate into real world electoral gains. The content that dominated social media feeds rarely addressed the concerns of key demographics like rural, working-class, and older voters. Instead, these platforms primarily catered to younger, urban, and progressive audiences who were already part of the Democratic coalition. The curated narratives presented a skewed reality, reinforcing the party's confidence in a strategy that ultimately left significant portions of the electorate feeling ignored.

Writing for *The Atlantic*, journalist David Frum encapsulated the phenomenon, stating, "Social media didn't just distort reality for voters, it distorted it for Democratic leaders, who mistook digital applause for genuine voter enthusiasm" (Frum, 2024). This distortion created a feedback loop where Democratic strategists, buoyed by the overwhelming visibility of pro-Harris content online, dismissed early warning signs from grassroots organizers about discontent in battleground states. As a result, the campaign heavily relied on digital metrics and engagement as indicators of success, blind to the fact that these signals were largely confined to their core base.

Algorithms and Partisan Amplification

The algorithms driving platforms like Twitter, Instagram, and TikTok were not neutral arbiters of information; rather, they played an active role in shaping public perception, often amplifying partisan narratives. These algorithms were designed to prioritize content that generated high engagement, typically sensational, emotionally charged material. As a result, they funneled users into echo chambers that reinforced existing biases and created a lopsided view of the candidates. For Kamala Harris, this dynamic worked in her favor, with pro-Democratic content dominating feeds, while Republican messaging was often sidelined or suppressed.

Critics argued that the algorithms were effectively written to steer public perception in a single direction about each candidate. Content promoting Harris frequently celebrated her historic candidacy and progressive platform, portraying her as a unifying and aspirational figure. Viral hashtags like #MadamPresident and #Kamala2024, combined with posts from influencers and celebrities, painted a rosy picture of her campaign. Conversely, content about Donald Trump was overwhelmingly negative, focusing on controversies, legal troubles, and inflammatory rhetoric. Fact-checking segments and editorialized posts scrutinized Trump's every statement while leaving many of Harris's policy proposals unexamined.

This algorithmic bias created an uneven playing field, where the narratives surrounding each candidate were starkly different. Writing for *The Atlantic*, David Frum noted, "Social media algorithms didn't just magnify polarization; they actively curated the way each candidate was perceived. Harris was framed as the future, while Trump was framed as the problem" (Frum, 2024). The deliberate focus on amplifying these narratives left little room for nuance or balanced discussion, further distorting voters' understanding of the election.

The Role of Curated Algorithms in Voter Perception

The partisan amplification was not incidental; it was the product of algorithms designed to prioritize engagement over accuracy. Posts that aligned with progressive talking points were rewarded with higher visibility, while conservative narratives often faced suppression. Reports from whistleblowers within major tech companies revealed that content moderation policies and algorithmic adjustments were implemented in ways that disproportionately de-prioritized right-leaning content during the campaign. While these measures were ostensibly designed to combat misinformation, they contributed to a perception among conservative voters that tech platforms were actively working against them.

For instance, a study conducted by the Media Research Center found that content promoting Democratic initiatives appeared 40% more frequently in user feeds compared to Republican messages, even when engagement levels were similar (MRC, 2024). This disparity was particularly evident on TikTok and Instagram, where short, visually appealing content celebrating Harris and mocking Trump went viral with regularity. Meanwhile, posts highlighting Republican perspectives on inflation, job creation, or energy policy struggled to gain traction, often flagged or buried by algorithms under the guise of community standards.

This curated digital environment shaped voter perceptions in profound ways. For younger, urban, and progressive users, the core demographics of platforms like Instagram and TikTok, the overwhelming visibility of pro-Harris content created the illusion of a Democratic landslide. However, these curated narratives failed to resonate with rural, working-class, and older voters, whose concerns about economic stability and cultural shifts were largely absent from the platforms' algorithms.

The Algorithm Isn't Your Friend

The algorithms' focus on amplifying one-sided narratives had tangible consequences for both the candidates and the electorate. Harris's campaign leaned heavily on the digital dominance fostered by these platforms, mistaking online applause for real-world voter enthusiasm. This overreliance on social media metrics blinded Democratic strategists to warning signs from battleground states, where concerns about inflation, healthcare, and energy policy were driving voter sentiment. By the time these issues gained national attention, it was too late to recalibrate the campaign's messaging.

For Trump, the algorithmic bias contributed to a narrative of persecution that energized his base. Conservative voters, already skeptical of mainstream media and tech platforms, rallied around the idea that the system was stacked against their candidate. The perceived manipulation of digital discourse became a talking point in Republican messaging, further solidifying their support among disaffected demographics.

The partisan amplification also deepened polarization, as users were rarely exposed to opposing viewpoints. Instead, the algorithms reinforced tribalism, making meaningful debate and cross-party understanding increasingly rare. The curated narratives left voters ill-equipped to engage with the complexity of the candidates' policies, reducing the election to a battle of perceptions rather than substance.

Lessons for Future Campaigns

The role of algorithms in shaping voter perception underscores the urgent need for greater transparency and accountability in how social media platforms operate during elections. While these platforms can mobilize specific demographics effectively, their ability to distort reality and amplify partisan divides poses significant risks to democratic processes. Future campaigns must recognize the limitations and biases of social media metrics, balancing digital strategies with substantive engagement that reaches beyond echo chambers.

For voters, the 2024 election serves as a reminder to critically evaluate the information presented on social media and seek out diverse sources of news. For policymakers, the election highlights the need for reforms that ensure algorithms prioritize balanced discourse over engagement-driven polarization.

By addressing the structural issues within these platforms and fostering a more inclusive digital environment, future elections can move closer to reflecting the genuine will of the people rather than the curated narratives of tech companies.

The Disconnect Between Social Media and Electoral Reality

Social media's influence on the 2024 election highlighted a fundamental disconnect between online narratives and electoral reality. Platforms like Instagram and TikTok were highly effective at mobilizing enthusiasm within Democratic strongholds but did little to bridge the cultural and economic divides that ultimately decided the election. Rural and working-class voters, critical to Republican victories in key swing states, were largely absent from the progressive-dominated digital discourse. Their concerns, including inflation, energy policy, and manufacturing jobs, were overshadowed by the social justice themes that dominated online platforms.

This disconnect was compounded by the Democratic campaign's overreliance on social media to gauge voter sentiment. The campaign mistook high engagement metrics and trending hashtags as evidence of broad-based support, ignoring warnings from field organizers and local leaders in battleground states. For instance, organizers in Pennsylvania and Wisconsin reported waning enthusiasm among blue-collar voters' months before the election, but these concerns were dismissed in favor of digital strategies that catered to urban progressives.

As a result, the Democratic Party entered election night confident in a strategy that had failed to resonate with large swaths of the electorate. The viral success of pro-Harris content created a false sense of security, blinding the campaign to the underlying discontent among key demographics. This miscalculation proved costly, as Republicans successfully mobilized rural, working-class, and suburban voters to deliver a decisive victory.

Lessons for Future Campaigns

The role of social media in the 2024 election underscores the need for political campaigns to move beyond the echo chambers of digital platforms and engage with the full spectrum of the electorate. While platforms like Twitter, Instagram, and TikTok are powerful tools for mobilizing younger and progressive voters, they cannot substitute for comprehensive outreach strategies that address the concerns of rural, working-class, and independent voters.

Campaigns must recognize the limitations of algorithms that prioritize sensational content and work to create messaging that resonates across demographic and geographic divides. Additionally, addressing perceptions of bias on these platforms will be crucial for restoring trust among conservative voters and fostering a more balanced political discourse.

In the end, the 2024 election serves as a cautionary tale about the dangers of relying too heavily on social media to shape political narratives. While these platforms can amplify messages and energize base voters, they must be balanced with on-the-ground efforts and substantive engagement to build the broad coalitions needed for electoral success.

From Echo Chamber to Election Loss

The combined influence of mainstream media and social media in the 2024 election fundamentally distorted the Democratic Party's perception of the political landscape. The dominant narrative, crafted by outlets like CNN, MSNBC, and *The New York Times*, along with viral social media trends, heavily emphasized cultural milestones, identity politics, and celebrity endorsements. While these strategies resonated with urban progressives and younger voters, they alienated significant portions of the electorate in economically vulnerable regions. Voters in rural areas and the working class felt sidelined, perceiving that their bread-and-butter issues—rising inflation, stagnant wages, and job insecurity—were not prioritized.

Mainstream media's treatment of the candidates further exacerbated this disconnect. Kamala Harris was celebrated in glowing terms, with interviews and coverage focusing on her historic candidacy and her role as a symbol of progress. Meanwhile, Donald Trump faced unrelenting scrutiny, with segments dissecting his rhetoric, legal troubles, and policy missteps. This disparity reinforced perceptions of bias among conservative and moderate voters. As one Wisconsin voter put it in an exit poll, "It felt like the media was campaigning for Harris while tearing Trump apart." This imbalance was not lost on voters; exit polls revealed that 68% of rural voters and 62% of working-class voters believed that mainstream media had an overt liberal bias (Pew Research Center, 2024).

Social media platforms like Twitter, Instagram, and TikTok further amplified this dynamic, creating curated echo chambers that projected an illusion of overwhelming Democratic support. Viral hashtags like #MadamPresident and #Kamala2024 dominated online discourse, reinforcing a narrative of inevitability that failed to translate into real-world momentum. Algorithms prioritized sensational content and progressive talking points, sidelining the economic concerns that were central to voters in battleground states like Pennsylvania, Wisconsin, and Arizona. For many, this digital environment symbolized the growing cultural divide between coastal elites and the rest of the nation.

The result was a narrative of elitism and disconnect that became deeply associated with the Democratic Party. By focusing on Harris's strengths and attacking Trump's weaknesses, the media inadvertently validated conservative claims of systemic bias and coastal elitism. Republican campaigns capitalized on this sentiment, framing themselves as the voice of "real Americans" fighting against an out-of-touch establishment. These perceptions galvanized Republican turnout, particularly among rural and working-class voters, solidifying the GOP's sweeping victory across the electoral map.

A Turning Point

The 2024 election was more than a defeat for the Democratic Party; it was a moment of reckoning that exposed deep structural and strategic flaws. The decision to replace Joe Biden with Kamala Harris was emblematic of the party's overconfidence and miscalculation of voter priorities. Intended to project a vision of progress and diversity, the move instead alienated voters who saw the decision as an elite-driven maneuver that ignored their voices. This perception was exacerbated by a campaign heavily reliant on celebrity endorsements and progressive social messaging, which failed to resonate with voters facing economic hardship.

Prominent Democratic leaders, including Nancy Pelosi, Elizabeth Warren, and Kamala Harris herself, bore the brunt of post-election criticism. Pelosi, as a longtime leader of the party, was accused of steering the Democrats further into a coastal, elite-driven identity that ignored working-class concerns. Warren, while vocal about economic issues, was criticized for not effectively counterbalancing the party's overemphasis on identity politics. Harris, the face of the campaign, became a lightning rod for criticism about the party's inability to connect with the broader electorate.

The fallout was immediate and far-reaching. Progressive factions within the party blamed centrists for failing to deliver bold economic reforms that could have energized the base, while moderates argued that the focus on social justice issues alienated swing voters in critical states. These divisions highlighted a party increasingly out of sync with a diverse and evolving electorate.

Compounding the internal strife was the sheer scale of the Republican victory. The GOP's success extended beyond the White House, as they secured control of the House and Senate, cementing a legislative majority that gave them unparalleled leverage. Even more striking was the Republican win of the popular vote, a feat that underscored the extent to which the Democrats had misjudged national sentiment. This comprehensive defeat signaled a profound shift in the political landscape, forcing Democrats to confront the structural weaknesses that had led to their downfall.

Looking ahead, rebuilding trust and credibility will require a fundamental reassessment of the Democratic Party's strategy and priorities. Leaders must address the economic concerns of working-class and rural voters, reinvest in grassroots organizing, and move beyond an overreliance on media and celebrity narratives. The lessons of 2024 will likely shape the party's approach for years to come, serving as a cautionary tale about the dangers of overconfidence, misjudged priorities, and ignoring the pulse of the nation. This election was not just a loss; it was a clear message from the electorate that cannot be ignored if the Democrats hope to remain a viable political force in the years to come.

The 2024 election laid bare the chasm between the Democratic Party's leadership and the electorate, a divide exacerbated by media narratives and digital echo chambers that prioritized optics over substance. While the campaign focused on historic milestones, cultural symbols, and celebrity endorsements, it failed to address the bread-and-butter issues that mattered most to voters in economically vulnerable and culturally distinct regions. The media's overt bias and social media's algorithmic amplification of partisan rhetoric compounded this disconnect, creating an illusion of widespread support that collapsed under the weight of voter realities.

For the Democratic Party, the election was not merely a defeat, it was a repudiation of a strategy that overestimated symbolic gestures and underestimated the electorate's frustrations with Washington. The sweeping Republican victory, from the White House to Congress and even the popular vote, served as a stark reminder of the perils of ignoring the pulse of the nation. The lessons of 2024 are clear: reconnecting with voters, addressing their tangible concerns, and breaking free from insular narratives are not just necessary, they are imperative for the party's survival in an increasingly polarized political landscape.

Chapter 14

What Went Wrong

The 2024 election was a profound reckoning for the Democratic Party, exposing deep flaws in its campaign messaging, strategy, and voter outreach. What was initially envisioned as a historic campaign to solidify Democratic dominance instead became a case study in political miscalculation, disconnection, and overconfidence. This chapter explores the synthesis of these failings and offers reflections from party insiders and critics on the missed opportunities that led to one of the most sweeping Republican victories in modern history.

Messaging: A Disconnect from the Electorate

At the heart of the Democratic campaign's failures was a messaging strategy that prioritized symbolic victories and progressive ideals over addressing the tangible, immediate concerns of everyday voters. The campaign's emphasis on Kamala Harris's historic candidacy as the first Black woman and Asian American to lead a major party ticket became a central narrative. While this milestone was undeniably significant and resonated with the party's urban, progressive base, it alienated key voter blocs, including rural communities, suburban moderates, and working-class Americans. These groups felt the campaign focused more on symbolic representation than on addressing their pressing economic realities.

Misalignment with Voter Priorities

The Democratic platform highlighted issues like climate justice, healthcare reform, and racial equity, critical topics with long-term societal implications. However, the campaign failed to frame these issues in a way that connected them to the immediate, everyday struggles of many Americans. In economically vulnerable regions, where families faced skyrocketing inflation, stagnant wages, and increasing job insecurity, these broader policy goals seemed disconnected from urgent local concerns. Exit polls revealed that 58% of voters ranked the economy as their top concern, yet the Democratic campaign devoted disproportionately more attention to social justice issues than to pragmatic economic solutions (Pew Research Center, 2024).

For example, the Democratic Party's proposals to transition to renewable energy were framed as a necessary step to combat climate change, but they were perceived in coal and manufacturing communities as a direct threat to their livelihoods. Voters in Rust Belt states, whose towns rely heavily on traditional industries, felt dismissed by rhetoric that championed environmental policies without acknowledging the economic displacement they could cause. As one factory worker in Pennsylvania told *Politico*, "I don't care what the energy of the future looks like if I can't afford groceries today" (Caputo, 2024; Miller & Franklin, 2024).

Similarly, while healthcare reform was a cornerstone of the Democratic platform, the messaging emphasized long-term structural changes rather than addressing the immediate challenges of affordability and access that voters face. For working-class families struggling to balance medical bills with rising costs of living, the campaign's broader narratives felt disconnected from their urgent needs.

The Role of Identity Politics

The Democratic campaign leaned heavily into identity politics, emphasizing cultural milestones over substantive economic solutions. Harris's candidacy was framed as a symbol of progress, with campaign messaging often centering on themes of representation and diversity. While these messages resonated deeply with urban, college-educated, and progressive voters, they alienated others who felt the campaign was overly focused on optics rather than addressing real-world problems.

This overemphasis on identity politics was particularly damaging among suburban moderates and rural voters, who often perceive such messaging as exclusionary or out of touch with their cultural and economic realities. For example, campaign ads highlighting Harris's cultural significance and celebrity endorsements were widely praised in progressive circles but failed to address the concerns of voters in economically distressed regions. "They talked about making history," said a voter in Michigan, "but what about making my life better?" (Smith, 2024).

Over-Reliance on Social Media and Celebrity Culture

The campaign's reliance on celebrity endorsements and viral social media content further compounded its messaging problems. Hashtags like #MadamPresident and #Kamala2024 dominated platforms like Twitter and Instagram, creating an illusion of widespread enthusiasm. While these trends energized younger, urban voters, they failed to engage voters outside urban centers and coastal states, where economic anxieties overshadowed cultural milestones.

The prominence of celebrity endorsements often distracted from substantive policy discussions. Figures like Taylor Swift, Beyoncé, and LeBron James drew significant attention to the campaign but also reinforced a perception of elitism and detachment from everyday concerns. Rural and working-class voters, who were struggling with inflation and job insecurity, found these endorsements irrelevant at best and condescending at worst. "They sent celebrities to talk to us like we're stupid," a Wisconsin farmer said in an interview with *The Wall Street Journal*. "What we need are leaders who actually listen to us" (Frum, 2024).

This inward-focused messaging strategy created a damaging echo chamber, where the campaign's digital success was mistaken for broad-based voter support. As one political strategist noted, "The Democrats were speaking to themselves, not to the voters they needed to win" (Caputo, 2024; Miller & Franklin, 2024). The party's leadership failed to recognize that online metrics like likes and retweets were not reflective of on-the-ground realities, particularly in battleground states where voter priorities were often vastly different from those amplified on social media.

Echo Chamber Effect

The Democratic campaign's reliance on progressive media outlets and social media platforms insulated it from criticism and constructive feedback. Outlets like CNN, MSNBC, and *The New York Times* often amplified the campaign's messaging without critically analyzing its shortcomings. Social media platforms further reinforced this dynamic, as algorithms prioritized content that generated engagement, often polarizing or sensational material. This approach gave the campaign a false sense of security, as digital applause was mistaken for voter enthusiasm.

David Frum, writing for *The Atlantic*, observed, "Social media didn't just distort reality for voters, it distorted it for Democratic leaders, who mistook digital applause for genuine voter enthusiasm" (Frum, 2024). This feedback loop blinded the campaign to the concerns of voters in rural and economically struggling regions, who felt left behind by both the party and its messaging.

Strategy: Overconfidence and Misallocation of Resources

The Democratic Party's strategic missteps were rooted in a dangerous overconfidence that underestimated the strength of Republican opposition and the discontent of swing-state voters. Internal polling, which consistently showed narrow Democratic leads in key battlegrounds like Pennsylvania, Wisconsin, and Arizona, lulled party leaders into a false sense of security. This confidence led to critical misallocations of resources, with heavy investments in urban centers and coastal strongholds while neglecting rural and economically struggling regions (Smith, 2024).

In battleground states, Democratic field operations were notably underfunded and understaffed. Reports from local organizers in Michigan and Wisconsin indicated a lack of door-to-door canvassing efforts and insufficient outreach to undecided voters. Instead, the campaign focused on high-profile events and digital outreach, which failed to engage communities that rely on face-to-face interactions to build trust. This neglect allowed the Republican campaign to dominate the ground game, deploying volunteers and resources to rural counties and suburban districts where their message of economic stability and cultural conservatism resonated strongly.

Additionally, the decision to replace Joe Biden with Kamala Harris as the nominee, though framed as a bold move, introduced its own set of challenges. While Harris's historic candidacy energized certain segments of the Democratic base, it also alienated others who viewed the decision as a top-down maneuver that disregarded voter input. Many moderates and swing voters were skeptical of Harris's ability to lead on critical issues like the economy and foreign policy, a concern that the campaign failed to address effectively (Frum, 2024). Instead of building a coalition around shared economic concerns, the campaign doubled down on progressive ideals that lacked universal appeal.

Voter Outreach: Failing to Meet the Moment

The Democratic Party's outreach efforts suffered from a fundamental misreading of voter priorities and a failure to engage critical demographics. Rural voters, who had long felt ignored by Democratic leadership, turned out in record numbers for the Republican candidate. This shift was driven by a perception that Democratic policies, particularly on energy and environmental issues, were dismissive of rural livelihoods. In states like Pennsylvania and Arizona, policies aimed at transitioning away from fossil fuels were seen as direct threats to industries that sustain entire communities.

Working-class voters, traditionally a cornerstone of the Democratic coalition, also drifted toward the Republican Party. These voters cited concerns about rising costs of living, job security, and the perceived disconnect between Democratic leadership and their everyday struggles. Exit polls showed that 62% of voters without a college degree favored the Republican candidate, reflecting a growing cultural and economic divide between the party and its historical base (Pew Research Center, 2024).

Even suburban voters, who had leaned Democratic in recent cycles, showed signs of reversion. Concerns about rising crime, education, and inflation drove many moderates back into the Republican fold. This trend was particularly pronounced in key districts in Wisconsin and Arizona, where Republican messaging on these issues outpaced Democratic responses (Caputo, 2024; Miller & Franklin, 2024).

The reliance on social media as a primary tool for voter engagement further compounded these outreach failures. Platforms like Twitter and Instagram amplified progressive talking points but failed to reach or persuade undecided voters in battleground states. While younger, urban voters were energized by viral content, this enthusiasm did not translate into the voter turnout needed to counteract Republican gains in rural and suburban areas (Frum, 2024).

Reflections from Insiders and Critics

In the aftermath of the election, Democratic leaders, strategists, and grassroots activists embarked on a period of intense reflection and critique, both publicly and privately, to identify the reasons behind their defeat. Prominent party figures, including Elizabeth Warren and Nancy Pelosi, voiced sharp criticisms regarding the party's failure to adequately address pressing economic concerns. Warren, in an interview with *The Washington Post*, underscored the disconnect, stating, "We need to stop talking at voters and start listening to them" (Smith, 2024). Pelosi echoed these sentiments, emphasizing the need for a more grounded approach to voter engagement.

At the grassroots level, frustration bubbled over, with organizers lamenting the disconnect between national leadership and local realities. A field organizer from Pennsylvania, speaking to *Politico*, expressed exasperation: "We warned them. We said inflation and jobs were the issues people cared about. But the campaign was too focused on its narrative to listen" (Miller & Franklin, 2024). This sentiment highlighted a growing divide between the party's central messaging and the concerns voiced by voters on the ground.

Meanwhile, conservative commentators seized the opportunity to frame the election results as a triumph of Republican principles and a repudiation of liberal elitism. Charles C.W. Cooke, writing for the *National Review*, argued that the Democrats' loss was not due to external factors like voter apathy or Republican machinations, but rather their own failure to remain attuned to the needs of their constituents. "The Democrats didn't lose because of voter apathy or Republican trickery. They lost because they stopped paying attention to the people they claimed to represent" (Frum, 2024).

The confluence of these perspectives painted a stark picture of a party grappling with its missteps and the challenges of reconnecting with a frustrated electorate.

Finally, the 2024 election stands as a sobering lesson for the Democratic Party, a moment of reckoning that underscores the consequences of losing touch with the electorate's most pressing concerns. While historic milestones and progressive ideals hold their place in shaping the future, they cannot come at the expense of addressing the immediate and tangible struggles faced by everyday Americans. The Democratic Party's missteps in messaging, strategy, and voter outreach reflect a broader need for introspection and recalibration. To move forward, the party must bridge the gap between ideals and realities, rebuild trust with disillusioned voters, and prioritize solutions that resonate across diverse communities. The road to recovery will require not just a change in tactics but a renewed commitment to listening, understanding, and delivering on the promises that truly matter to those they aspire to represent. Only then can they hope to turn defeat into a foundation for future success.

Chapter 15

The Future of the Democratic Party

The Democratic Party faces a critical juncture as it grapples with the fallout from its 2024 electoral defeat. While the immediate aftermath has been one of introspection, moving forward requires strategic vision and decisive action. This chapter examines the steps the Democratic Party must take to regain its footing in future elections and the implications of a political landscape increasingly dominated by independent voters and waning party loyalty.

Regaining Footing: Strategic Priorities for Future Elections

1. Rebuilding Economic Credibility

Economic issues consistently rank as the most pressing concerns for voters, as evidenced by the 2024 election, where inflation and job insecurity overshadowed other policy priorities (Pew Research Center, 2024). To regain its footing, the Democratic Party must prioritize policies that directly address economic challenges while effectively communicating their benefits to voters. Key areas of focus include:

- Tackling Inflation and Cost of Living: Democrats should articulate clear plans to combat inflation, reduce energy costs, and improve access to affordable housing. Policies that resonate with middle-class families, such as childcare tax credits and protections for Social Security, could help rebuild trust with economically vulnerable demographics (Smith, 2024).

- Investing in Local Economies: The party must pivot from broad economic promises to targeted investments in communities. Initiatives that support small businesses, bolster vocational training, and revive industries in rural and Rust Belt regions are essential for reestablishing connections with disaffected voters (Caputo, 2024; Miller & Franklin, 2024).

- Balancing Progressive and Pragmatic Policies: While issues like climate change and healthcare reform are central to the Democratic platform, they must be framed through the lens of economic opportunity. For example, promoting clean energy jobs as replacements for traditional industries can help address voter concerns about economic displacement (Frum, 2024).

2. Reconnecting with Rural and Working-Class Voters

The 2024 election highlighted the Democratic Party's growing disconnect with rural and working-class communities. These groups, which historically formed the backbone of the party's coalition, increasingly perceive Democratic policies as dismissive of their cultural and economic realities. To bridge this divide, Democrats need to:

- Engage in Active Listening: Democratic candidates and leaders must spend more time in rural areas, holding town halls and listening sessions to understand voters' concerns. This approach demonstrates a willingness to engage beyond election cycles (Vincent, 2024).

- Adapt Messaging to Local Contexts: National campaigns often fail to resonate with local audiences. Tailoring messages to reflect the unique challenges and opportunities within specific regions can help the party regain credibility.

- Respect Cultural Values: Addressing cultural issues with sensitivity and avoiding perceived elitism or moral superiority will be critical. Policies should be framed in ways that affirm shared values rather than exacerbating divisions.

3. Leveraging Data and Technology for Outreach

In an increasingly digital age, the Democratic Party must refine its use of data and technology to enhance voter engagement. However, the 2024 campaign revealed the dangers of over-reliance on social media metrics that fail to translate into electoral success (Frum, 2024). Moving forward, Democrats should:

- Invest in Ground Campaigns: Door-to-door canvassing and face-to-face interactions remain some of the most effective ways to mobilize voters. Strengthening grassroots operations can help counter Republican dominance in ground-game efforts (Caputo, 2024; Miller & Franklin, 2024).

- Bridge the Digital Divide: While urban and younger voters are well-represented online, rural and older demographics often rely on traditional media. Developing a multi-channel communication strategy ensures broader reach.

4. Reinforcing Party Unity

Internal divisions within the Democratic Party, between progressives and moderates, hampered its ability to present a cohesive message in 2024. To avoid similar pitfalls, the party must prioritize unity through:

- Inclusive Policymaking: Bringing together diverse factions within the party to craft a shared vision will strengthen internal cohesion.

- Focus on Common Ground: Emphasizing universal issues like economic security and healthcare reform can help bridge ideological divides.

The Rise of Independent Voters and the Decline of Party Loyalty

1. Understanding the Independent Voter Surge

Independent voters now represent a significant and growing portion of the electorate, accounting for approximately 40% of registered voters as of 2024 (Pew Research Center, 2024). This demographic shift reflects widespread disillusionment with the two-party system and poses unique challenges and opportunities for both major parties.

- Disaffection with Partisan Politics: Many independents cite dissatisfaction with hyper-partisanship, gridlock, and perceived corruption within both parties as reasons for their disaffiliation. The Democratic Party must address these concerns by emphasizing transparency and bipartisanship (Vincent, 2024).

- Diverse Ideologies: Unlike traditional party loyalists, independents are not a monolithic group. They range from fiscally conservative but socially liberal voters to progressive-leaning individuals who reject party labels. Understanding this diversity is critical for effective outreach (Smith, 2024).

2. Strategies for Engaging Independent Voters

To appeal to independents, the Democratic Party must adopt a more flexible and inclusive approach:

- Focus on Problem-Solving Over Ideology: Independents are often pragmatic voters who prioritize effective governance over ideological purity. Democrats should highlight their commitment to results-driven policies that address issues like infrastructure, healthcare, and economic stability.

- Offer Moderate Candidates: While progressives play a vital role in energizing the party base, centrist candidates may have broader appeal among independents in competitive districts and swing states (Frum, 2024).

- Address the Partisan Divide: Promoting initiatives that foster bipartisanship and reduce polarization can resonate with independents who are weary of political infighting.

3. Rebuilding Trust in Institutions

The erosion of trust in political institutions is a driving factor behind the rise of independents. To counter this trend, Democrats must:

- Champion Electoral Reforms: Advocating for measures like ranked-choice voting and campaign finance reform can demonstrate a commitment to improving democracy.

- Enhance Civic Engagement: Encouraging voter participation through education and outreach can help rebuild confidence in the electoral process.

4. Preparing for a Post-Party Era

As party loyalty continues to decline, the Democratic Party must adapt to a political landscape where voters prioritize issues and candidates over party affiliation. This shift requires:

- Building Broad Coalitions: Focusing on shared values and common goals can help the party attract a wider range of voters.

- Emphasizing Local Leadership: Strengthening state and local party organizations ensures that candidates are more attuned to the needs of their communities.

The Democratic Party stands at a crossroads, facing a critical opportunity to redefine its identity and strategy in an era marked by shifting voter loyalties and growing independence from traditional partisan structures. To secure its future, the party must listen more deeply, engage more broadly, and act more decisively on the issues that matter most to Americans. Rebuilding trust with rural and working-class voters, bridging ideological divides, and crafting a message that resonates across the diverse fabric of the electorate are not just goals, they are imperatives. Simultaneously, the rise of independent voters signals a need for adaptability, pragmatism, and a renewed commitment to bipartisan problem-solving. By addressing these challenges head-on, the Democratic Party can transform its 2024 defeat into a catalyst for meaningful change, ensuring it remains a vital force in shaping the future of American democracy.

Chapter 16

The Role of Celebrities in Politics

The influence of celebrity culture on political campaigns has grown significantly in recent decades, culminating in a political landscape where public figures from entertainment and sports frequently participate in shaping voter sentiment. While celebrities can amplify campaign messages and draw attention to critical issues, their involvement raises important questions about the role of celebrity culture in serious political discourse. Does their influence dilute the focus on policy, or does it provide a necessary bridge to disengaged voters? This chapter critically examines whether celebrity endorsements and activism are beneficial to the political process and explores the potential for a return to grassroots, policy-driven politics as a counterweight to the growing spectacle of celebrity involvement.

The Influence of Celebrity Culture on Political Campaigns

Celebrity endorsements have long been a feature of American politics, but their prominence has expanded significantly in the 21st century. High-profile figures have championed political causes and candidates, using their immense platforms to rally support and energize specific demographics. The advantages of celebrity endorsements are clear. They bring visibility to campaigns, infuse them with cultural relevance, and often mobilize younger, tech-savvy voters who may otherwise feel disconnected from traditional political processes. For example, in the 2024 election, Taylor Swift's voter registration campaign reportedly led to a surge in new registrations among millennials and Gen Z, showcasing the tangible impact of celebrity-driven activism (Pew Research Center, 2024).

However, this influence is not without its drawbacks. Critics argue that an over-reliance on celebrities shifts the focus away from substantive policy debates and reduces complex political discussions to simplified soundbites. This was evident in the 2024 election, where hashtags like #Kamala2024 trended widely on social media but failed to address voter concerns about economic instability and inflation (Smith, 2024). Celebrity endorsements often create a perception of elitism, reinforcing the idea that politics has become a spectacle dominated by out-of-touch figures with little understanding of the struggles faced by average Americans. This criticism was particularly pronounced in rural communities, where voters expressed frustration with celebrity surrogates sent to campaign on behalf of candidates. A farmer in Wisconsin commented, "They sent celebrities to talk to us like we're stupid. What we need are leaders who actually listen to us" (Caputo, 2024).

Social media has further amplified the role of celebrities in politics. Platforms like Twitter, Instagram, and TikTok allow public figures to directly engage with millions of followers, bypassing traditional media channels. While this has democratized access to political discourse, it has also contributed to the creation of echo chambers where messages are tailored to resonate within specific audiences rather than addressing the broader electorate. Viral content, often promoted by celebrity endorsements, garners likes and shares but does not necessarily translate into voter turnout or meaningful engagement with policy issues (Frum, 2024). This reliance on digital metrics creates an illusion of widespread support, masking deeper issues of voter alienation and disconnection from campaign priorities.

The growing influence of celebrity culture raises critical questions about its place in serious political campaigns. While celebrities bring visibility and energy to campaigns, their involvement often overshadows the substantive discussions necessary for informed decision-making. Balancing the benefits of celebrity endorsements with the need for policy-driven discourse is essential for preserving the integrity of democratic processes.

Case for a Return to Grassroots, Policy-Driven Politics

The increasing prominence of celebrity culture in politics has coincided with growing voter dissatisfaction with campaigns that prioritize spectacle over substance. This presents a compelling case for a return to grassroots, policy-driven politics, which emphasizes direct engagement with voters, community-level organizing, and a focus on tangible solutions to pressing issues. Grassroots campaigns have historically been a cornerstone of American democracy, fostering trust and participation by addressing local concerns and building authentic connections between candidates and constituents.

One of the primary benefits of grassroots politics is its ability to rebuild trust in a political system that many voters perceive as out of touch with their needs. By engaging directly with communities through town halls, door-to-door canvassing, and listening sessions, grassroots campaigns demonstrate a genuine commitment to understanding and addressing voter priorities. This approach contrasts sharply with the top-down nature of celebrity-driven campaigns, which often appear disconnected from the realities of everyday life for many Americans (Vincent, 2024).

Grassroots campaigns also prioritize policy over personalities, offering voters detailed proposals and actionable solutions to their most pressing concerns. This was exemplified by Barack Obama's 2008 campaign, which relied heavily on grassroots organizing and small donor contributions to mobilize millions of first-time voters. Similarly, Bernie Sanders' presidential campaigns in 2016 and 2020 showcased the power of policy-driven messaging to energize young and working-class voters (Street, 2019). These examples highlight the enduring appeal of grassroots strategies in fostering meaningful political engagement.

Despite its potential, a return to grassroots politics faces significant challenges in the modern media landscape. The dominance of social media and the immediacy of digital communication make it difficult for grassroots campaigns to compete with the viral appeal of celebrity-driven narratives. Campaigns must navigate the tension between traditional organizing methods and the need to engage voters on digital platforms. Additionally, grassroots organizing requires substantial resources, including funding for field operations and staffing, which can strain campaign budgets (Caputo, 2024; Miller & Franklin, 2024).

Another obstacle to grassroots politics is the erosion of voter trust in political institutions. Decades of partisan gridlock and perceived corruption have left many voters skeptical of grassroots promises, viewing them as little more than rhetorical tools. To overcome this cynicism, campaigns must prioritize transparency and accountability, demonstrating a commitment to delivering on their policy proposals and addressing the needs of their communities.

While these challenges are formidable, they are not insurmountable. A return to grassroots, policy-driven politics offers a pathway to restoring faith in the political process and re-centering campaigns on the issues that matter most to voters. By prioritizing authenticity, inclusivity, and substantive engagement, grassroots strategies can counter the spectacle of celebrity culture and reinvigorate democratic participation.

Balancing Celebrity Influence and Grassroots Principles

The role of celebrities in politics is a reflection of broader cultural trends that prioritize visibility and entertainment in the public sphere. While celebrity endorsements can bring attention to important issues and mobilize specific demographics, they often risk overshadowing the substantive policy discussions that are critical to informed democratic decision-making. The Democratic Party, and political campaigns more broadly, must strive to balance the benefits of celebrity involvement with the need for grassroots, policy-driven engagement. By reconnecting with voters at the community level and emphasizing practical solutions to their concerns, campaigns can counteract the pitfalls of celebrity culture and restore the integrity of political discourse. In doing so, they can create a political landscape that values substance over spectacle and empowers voters to shape their futures.

Chapter 17

Rebuilding the Republic

If American democracy is to be preserved and strengthened, it must begin with an overhaul of the very institutions that drive it: the Democratic and Republican national committees. For decades, both parties have drifted away from the democratic principles they claim to uphold. Party elites, insulated from public accountability, have increasingly made decisions behind closed doors, bypassing voter input in favor of insider politics. The 2024 Democratic nomination, where party leaders sidestepped the primary process to install Vice President Kamala Harris as the nominee, serves as a potent example of how party machinery can disenfranchise its base (Hilton, 2024).

Eliminate Backroom Coronations

Reinstating democratic norms begins with ending backroom coronations. The party apparatus must not override the will of voters by selecting candidates without a transparent and participatory primary process. Whether it be Republicans shielding incumbents from challengers or Democrats consolidating around a preordained nominee, the practice weakens public trust and participation. Every major candidate must be vetted through open debate, primary voting, and grassroots campaigning.

Increase Transparency in Delegate and Fundraising Processes

Delegate selection remains opaque to most voters. To rebuild confidence, both parties must simplify and disclose delegate allocation processes, providing real-time data and clear explanations of how delegates are awarded and pledged. Similarly, fundraising transparency should be mandated. The public deserves to know who is funding candidates, how much they contribute, and what influence those contributions might exert (Federal Election Commission, 2023).

Reinstate Grassroots Influence Over Candidate Selection

The heart of a democratic party lies in its grassroots. Candidate forums, town halls, and caucus-style input must be revived and expanded. Party platforms and candidate endorsements should reflect not just donor interests or media narratives, but the will of engaged citizens at the community level. State and local party organizations must play a larger role in shaping national candidate viability, rather than serving as mere rubber stamps for national leadership.

Breaking the Grip of the Donor Class

The influence of wealthy donors and corporate entities has reached a dangerous crescendo in American politics. Super PACs, dark money groups, and billion-dollar campaigns distort the electoral process and prioritize access over accountability. Both the DNC and GOP have been complicit in elevating the power of their biggest donors while ignoring the needs of average citizens.

Ban Dark Money and Super PAC Coordination

Dark money groups operate in the shadows, shielding donor identities and influencing elections without meaningful oversight. Congress must act to require full disclosure of all political contributions, including those funneled through 501(c)(4) organizations and other legal loopholes (Brennan Center for Justice, 2023). Furthermore, coordination between candidates and Super PACs should be explicitly prohibited and subject to strict enforcement. The current "wink-and-nod" relationship between campaigns and supposedly independent PACs has rendered existing laws toothless.

Enforce Contribution Caps and Public Financing Models

To level the playing field, strict contribution caps must be enforced. No individual or corporation should be able to buy disproportionate influence over a candidate or party. Public financing models, like those used in some state and municipal elections, have demonstrated that clean elections are possible when candidates are incentivized to raise money from a broad base of small-dollar donors. A federal matching program, for instance, could multiply donations under $200 and shift campaign strategies away from high-dollar fundraisers and toward grassroots engagement (Campaign Legal Center, 2024).

The future of American democracy depends on restoring integrity, equity, and access to the political process. Without bold reform to party structures and campaign finance, elections will continue to reflect the interests of the wealthy few rather than the will of the people.

Empowering the People: Electoral System Overhaul

Modern American democracy faces a fundamental challenge: a political system increasingly dominated by two entrenched parties that often prioritize loyalty and longevity over innovation and accountability. To truly revitalize representative government, structural reforms to our electoral system must be enacted. These changes are not about favoring one party or ideology but about expanding democratic participation, reducing polarization, and restoring trust in governance. Three crucial reforms stand out: ranked-choice voting, term limits for Congress, and enhanced ballot access for independent and third-party candidates.

Enact Ranked-Choice Voting Nationwide

Ranked-choice voting (RCV) allows voters to rank candidates in order of preference rather than selecting only one. If no candidate receives a majority of first-choice votes, the candidate with the fewest votes is eliminated, and their votes are redistributed based on voters' next preferences. This process continues until one candidate secures a majority.

RCV mitigates the "spoiler effect" that often plagues elections where third-party candidates draw votes away from major contenders, potentially altering outcomes in unintended ways. Instead of discouraging support for alternative candidates, RCV allows voters to express their true preferences without fear of wasting their vote (FairVote, 2023).

Additionally, RCV incentivizes candidates to appeal to a broader electorate to gain second- and third-choice votes. This fosters coalition-building and discourages hyper-partisanship. Studies of RCV in cities such as San Francisco and Minneapolis show that it leads to more civil campaigns and encourages greater voter satisfaction with outcomes (Donovan, Tolbert, & Gracey, 2019).

Institute Term Limits for Congress

America's Founding Fathers envisioned public service as a temporary civic duty, not a lifelong career. Yet today, Congress is populated by politicians who serve for decades, often growing more beholden to party elites and lobbyists than to their constituents. Instituting term limits for members of Congress would disrupt this pattern of entrenchment and open the door for fresh perspectives.

Term limits reduce the incentive for politicians to prioritize re-election above all else. By creating regular turnover, new leaders with innovative ideas can rise to power, and stagnant political cultures can be revitalized. Moreover, term limits are widely popular among American voters; a 2022 Pew Research Center poll found that 87% of respondents favored term limits for members of Congress (Pew Research Center, 2022).

Critics argue that term limits may reduce institutional knowledge, but this can be counterbalanced with stronger support for nonpartisan staff and institutional memory-building. Ultimately, the benefits of breaking the cycle of careerism outweigh the potential drawbacks.

Strengthen Ballot Access for Independent and Third-Party Candidates

The current electoral system strongly favors the two major parties through restrictive ballot access laws that make it difficult for independent and third-party candidates to compete. These barriers include high signature thresholds, onerous filing fees, and inconsistent rules that vary dramatically between states.

To encourage true competition and innovation in policy, reforms must ensure that qualified candidates outside the Democratic and Republican parties can reasonably appear on ballots. This would allow voters to consider a wider array of choices and force the major parties to be more responsive to shifting public demands.

Reforming ballot access laws would also reduce voter disenchantment. Many Americans do not feel fully represented by the two major parties. According to a 2024 Gallup poll, 62% of Americans believe a third major party is needed (Gallup, 2024). Facilitating greater participation by independents and minor parties can help restore faith in the electoral process and stimulate meaningful political dialogue.

Empowering the people begins with empowering their choices. Through ranked-choice voting, congressional term limits, and broader ballot access, America can reclaim the promise of its democratic system. These reforms will not solve every issue, but they lay a critical foundation for a more accountable, competitive, and representative political future.

Building a Grassroots Renaissance

Reinvigorating American democracy requires more than top-down reform—it demands a true grassroots renaissance. For decades, both major political parties have grown increasingly detached from everyday voters, relying on national media narratives and celebrity surrogates instead of cultivating local leadership. This chapter explores how we rebuild civic trust and political engagement from the ground up.

Invest in Local Leadership

Reviving democracy starts in city halls, school boards, and state legislatures. Local governance is where policies most directly affect citizens' lives, yet it is too often overlooked in national political discourse. Investing in local leadership means encouraging a new generation of leaders who are grounded in their communities and capable of addressing their unique needs (Han, 2014). Supporting local candidates with authentic connections to their neighborhoods fosters accountability and relevance in policymaking.

To create systemic change, national political organizations must prioritize training programs, mentoring networks, and accessible campaign resources for city council and school board candidates. Such investments not only diversify political representation but also build a pipeline of future leaders rooted in public service rather than ambition.

Reconnect With Working-Class America

The rift between political elites and working-class communities has grown dangerously wide. While cultural debates dominate headlines, kitchen-table concerns, like affordable healthcare, housing, and living wages remain unresolved. To win back trust, parties must stop posturing and start listening.

Leaders must elevate voices that speak directly to economic realities, not those trained in media spin. This means focusing campaign messaging on tangible improvements to everyday life rather than abstract ideological victories. Candidates who can relate to voters' financial struggles and lived experiences are far more likely to inspire turnout and trust (Cramer, 2016; Fiorina et al., 2011).

Coalition Building Across Divides

Real progress requires unity across ideological lines. From national debt and healthcare to education and the dignity of work, many issues transcend party boundaries. Political leaders and citizens alike must commit to building coalitions focused on shared priorities rather than partisan division.

Organizations like Braver Angels and More in Common have demonstrated that civil discourse and common ground are not only possible but essential to healing the national divide (Braver Angels, 2024). Investing in these efforts can shift the tone of politics from adversarial to cooperative, reminding Americans that they share more in common than they are led to believe.

A grassroots renaissance is not a nostalgic return to simpler politics, it is a strategic, community-driven effort to restore accountability, relevance, and trust in the democratic process. The future of American democracy depends not on celebrities or billionaires, but on everyday citizens taking ownership of their political destiny.

Detoxing Our Media and Digital Ecosystem

In an age where digital algorithms dictate public discourse and outrage is monetized, detoxifying America's media and information ecosystem is critical to rebuilding public trust and preserving democratic norms. The influence of online platforms and partisan media has distorted political realities, radicalized discourse, and driven Americans into echo chambers. Reforms are urgently needed to dismantle these digital incentives and restore credibility to information sources.

Regulate Algorithmic Amplification of Extremism

The architecture of social media platforms prioritizes engagement over accuracy, often amplifying divisive and sensational content to keep users glued to their screens. According to the Center for Humane Technology (2023), engagement-based algorithms contribute significantly to polarization by disproportionately recommending inflammatory and extreme content. To address this, Congress must demand transparency in algorithmic practices and require tech companies to disclose how their systems influence information dissemination and public sentiment (Tufekci, 2023).

Policies must also break the economic incentives that reward the spread of outrage. This includes revising Section 230 of the Communications Decency Act to hold platforms accountable when their algorithms intentionally promote harmful content. Regulation should prioritize public safety and civic integrity over advertising revenue, aligning technological growth with democratic stability.

Revive Journalism with Substance

The collapse of local journalism and the rise of hyper-partisan outlets have contributed to a national information crisis. Pew Research Center (2022) found that trust in media has reached historic lows, particularly among younger and rural Americans. To reverse this trend, governments and philanthropic organizations must invest in local and independent journalism that focuses on accountability reporting and fact-based analysis.

Public subsidies, similar to those used in Scandinavian countries, could help sustain nonpartisan newsrooms, while regulatory frameworks must discourage outlets that repeatedly spread disinformation. Outlets that thrive on partisan sensationalism should be held to higher standards of transparency and accuracy, with penalties for habitual dissemination of provably false content.

Promote Media Literacy in Education

Long-term resilience against disinformation requires systemic change in how Americans, especially young people, consume and evaluate information. Integrating media literacy into public education curricula is essential. Programs should teach students how to identify propaganda, understand bias, and verify sources, equipping the next generation to critically engage with digital content rather than passively absorb it (Hobbs, 2021).

By promoting media literacy, reviving substantive journalism, and reining in algorithmic extremism, America can take bold steps toward restoring trust in information and dismantling the digital scaffolding that props up misinformation and division.

Restoring Faith Through Civic Education and Accountability

The erosion of trust in American institutions is not just the result of partisan rhetoric or economic instability, it is also the product of an electorate increasingly distanced from the mechanisms of governance. A functioning democracy depends not only on informed voters but also on accountable leaders. Rebuilding that civic foundation will require bold, bipartisan reforms in education, transparency, and voter access.

National Civics Revamp

American civics education has long been neglected, with many states failing to require comprehensive instruction on the Constitution, civil rights, or the functioning of government (National Center for Education Statistics, 2022). According to a 2022 Annenberg Public Policy Center survey, only 47% of Americans could name all three branches of government; a startling reminder of the civic illiteracy that undercuts participatory democracy (Annenberg, 2022).

To address this, a national initiative is needed to revamp civics curricula in K–12 and higher education. This includes a nuanced approach to American history that acknowledges both triumphs and failures, mandatory instruction in constitutional principles, and digital media literacy to combat disinformation. A well-informed electorate is essential not only to voting but to holding power accountable across local, state, and federal levels.

Hold Elected Officials Accountable

Transparency must become a cornerstone of public office. Real-time disclosure of voting records, lobbying influences, and campaign spending should be mandatory and accessible to all citizens. Platforms such as OpenSecrets.org and GovTrack have taken steps in this direction, but without institutional mandates, accountability remains voluntary and incomplete (Center for Responsive Politics, 2023).

Congress should pass legislation requiring all elected officials to publicly disclose financial transactions, donor influence, and legislative negotiations in real time. Additionally, penalties for ethics violations must be enforced uniformly and without partisan bias. The public has the right to know not just how their representatives vote, but why.

Institute a Voter Empowerment Bill of Rights

Strengthening American democracy also means removing barriers to participation. A national Voter Empowerment Bill of Rights should include automatic voter registration at age 18, universal early voting access, and secure voter ID protocols that ensure both inclusion and integrity (Brennan Center for Justice, 2023). These policies would modernize the electoral system while maintaining trust and accessibility for all citizens.

Rather than endless court battles over voting rules, Congress should enact baseline standards that guarantee every eligible voter the opportunity to participate, regardless of state politics. Secure ID access does not mean suppression if implemented alongside free government-issued IDs and expanded registration infrastructure.

A Nation Worth Rebuilding

America doesn't need more performance, it needs purpose.
We've spent too long watching politics become a theater of the absurd, where celebrity soundbites replace substance and campaign ads matter more than policy. Our republic is being hollowed out not by foreign forces, but by domestic complacency.

Real reform will never come from the marble halls of Congress or the green rooms of cable news. It will rise from kitchen tables, community centers, and classrooms, from ordinary citizens who choose action over apathy. These reforms must be demanded from below, because those at the top are too busy protecting their seats to fix the foundation.

The future of this country will not be shaped by better actors, it will be saved by better citizens. And if we fail to rise to that challenge, history won't remember us as the generation that saved the republic.
It will remember us as the audience that applauded while it fell.

Chapter 18

The Death of Illusion, The Demand for Reality

The election did more than shift power—it shattered the illusion that spectacle, symbolism, and celebrity can substitute for substance. It exposed a raw and uncomfortable truth: America is not entertained, it's exhausted. The Democratic Party's fixation on star-studded rallies, viral soundbites, and curated identity politics failed to confront the one thing voters demanded most, reality. Rising inflation, unaffordable housing, stagnant wages, and a widening gap between the governed and the governing revealed a painful disconnect that no Hollywood cameo could conceal.

This failure wasn't a fluke, it was the natural result of a strategy that confused applause with trust and fame with connection. For too long, the Democratic Party relied on cultural capital and celebrity endorsements to win elections, assuming that charisma could carry them where policy no longer reached. But by placing image over integrity and performance over purpose, the party alienated the very voters it once claimed to champion, working-class Americans, rural communities, and disillusioned independents.

But this wasn't just a Democratic failing, it was a national reckoning. The political class, across the aisle, has traded town halls for TikToks, policy for performance, and purpose for applause. The result? A fractured electorate, disillusioned by leaders who mistake trending hashtags for transformative leadership. Campaigns flooded with digital dopamine might feed egos and news cycles, but they starve the very people they claim to serve. American democracy cannot survive as a stage show. And yet, both parties are acting like the lights will never go out.

Both parties have chosen theatrics over thoughtful governance. While Democrats leaned into cultural icons and viral moments, Republicans embraced outrage merchants and anti-establishment slogans with no follow-through. In both cases, the working class got theater—while their paychecks stayed flat.

Nowhere is that more obvious than in how they treat the national debt and the debt ceiling—not as existential threats to our economic future, but as weapons in their endless war for control. Each year, we watch the same scripted standoff: Republicans threaten to crash the economy in the name of fiscal discipline they rarely uphold; Democrats decry the danger, then sign off on more spending they can't justify. The debt ceiling becomes a political hostage, a media spectacle, a game of chicken with the future of the republic, while the real crisis goes ignored.

But there's a darker truth: the national debt isn't just neglected, it's being weaponized. Politicians use it to manipulate fear, justify cuts to programs they never liked, and consolidate power under the illusion of emergency. At the same time, the ultra-wealthy benefit from the chaos. They thrive on low interest rates, government bailouts, and inflation that quietly transfers wealth upward. Every trillion added to the debt buys time—for them. It inflates stock portfolios, props up markets, and preserves an economic system designed not to serve the many, but to shelter the few.

America's national debt as of April 4, 2025, is over $36 trillion and counting (U.S. Department of the Treasury, 2025). That's where we are. And still; no real plan. No accountability. No urgency. Just more borrowing, more printing, more pretending. Every new administration inherits a larger debt than the one before it, and every time, they promise "responsible budgeting" while quietly adding fuel to the fire. Both parties have made it clear: winning the next election is more important than saving the nation.

This is not just irresponsible. It's civilizational suicide. Empires don't collapse from one bad leader or one bad policy. They rot from within—when their elites become so drunk on spectacle and self-preservation that they lose touch with the governed. Rome didn't fall from invasion alone. It collapsed under the weight of endless spending, internal decay, and a ruling class too insulated to see the storm coming. So did Greece. So did the British Empire. So did the USSR.

And now, so might the mighty United States of America.

America's debt is not just an economic concern. It's a strategic vulnerability, a slow-bleeding wound that threatens our global standing, our domestic stability, and our future as the world's leading power. You cannot maintain strength, stability, or sovereignty while mortgaging your children's future to finance today's dysfunction. You cannot lead the world while buried in debt and dependent on foreign creditors.

Debt is a dagger at the heart of our global influence, a flashing sign of a nation living beyond its means and drifting toward decline. If we continue down this path, the world won't be shocked when America stumbles. It will be ready when we fall.

And let us not forget the role of America's cultural royalty: its celebrities. No matter their number, wealth, platform, or global influence, they are not here to save the Nation, the Union, the American democracy—they are here to protect their status. They may perform activism from a luxury suite or drop soundbites between press tours, but at the end of the day, their brand comes before your future. Their power comes from attention, not action. Their loyalty lies not with the country, but with their image. While the working class drowns in debt, they jet from award shows to fundraisers, draped in virtue while cashing checks in silence. They are not the voice of the people, they are the distraction from their suffering.

Worse still, many of them benefit from the same debt-fueled system, one that keeps markets hot, interest rates low, and government handouts flowing to the already powerful. In times of economic pain, the rich expand their empires while the average American tries to afford eggs.

This is the legacy of a politics built on spectacle. A party, once the champion of laborers, farmers, and working families, now seeks approval from influencers and red carpets. And while Democratic leaders praised celebrity surrogates for their passion, voters were left asking: "What about my mortgage? My job? My kid's future?"

Public trust is eroding, not from apathy, but from betrayal. Americans aren't asking for perfection; they're asking to be heard. They want leaders who don't talk at them from scripted stages but listen, really listen, from kitchen tables, factory floors, and small-town sidewalks. Yet both parties have grown comfortable in the warm glow of their echo chambers, where data is distorted, dissent is dismissed, and economic collapse is postponed just long enough to blame someone else.

I wore the uniform, built a business, and led in higher education, and I still believe in this country. But I've never seen trust this low. Not because Americans stopped caring, but because they're tired of being lied to by people who've never held a shovel, missed a rent payment, or carried a student loan.

Let the 2024 election be a final warning: optics cannot patch over outrage, and charisma cannot cancel consequences. Voters are no longer fooled by celebrity endorsements, empty slogans, or digital theatrics. They want, and deserve, action. This isn't a branding issue. This is a democratic crisis. An economic crisis. A spiritual one.

The path forward demands courage, not the kind that shows up on stage, but the kind that writes hard legislation, faces public anger, and tells the truth, even when it's unpopular. Policies must once again put people over donors, communities over algorithms, and truth over spin. Because if leaders continue to campaign like influencers and govern like technocrats, they will forfeit the one thing democracy cannot survive without: faith from the people

This is the moment. Strip away the spectacle. Smash the illusions. Burn the script. Rebuild trust with truth. Because if our politics remain a show, America is the one being played, and the curtain is already closing.

What Needs to Happen Now

America needs action, not more performance. Here's what must happen next:

- **Reclaim politics from performers.** Stop electing personalities. Start electing problem-solvers. Choose leaders who govern with integrity—not influencers who chase applause.

- **Demand fiscal accountability.** Force a real, transparent national conversation on spending, debt, and economic survival. Stop the borrowing binge before it bankrupts our future.

- **Reject the fame filter.** Don't let celebrities dictate public policy. They weren't elected. They're not experts. And their loyalty is to their brand—not your family.

- **Break the algorithmic echo chambers.** Challenge the digital silos that divide us. Push for media literacy in schools, and back leaders who prioritize truth over tribalism.

- **Revive civic courage.** Support those rare leaders who are willing to lose followers, face criticism, and make unpopular decisions if it means doing what's right for the country.

And when the final scene fades, there will be no encore. Only the silence of a republic that mistook celebrity friendships and cultural capital for leadership and fell while the world watched.

America is not dying from outside threats; it is being hollowed out from within by a political system bought by billionaires and blinded by celebrity worship. We've become a nation more captivated by Paris Hilton's out-of-control life, S. Diddy's disturbing behavior, Taylor Swift's next relationship, Kim Kardashian's latest photo shoot, and Leonardo DiCaprio's newest twenty-something girlfriend than by the American Dream of Justice, Liberty, and Freedom for all.

If we do not break this cycle of corruption, distraction, and decay, we will not merely echo the fall of past empires, we will redefine it.

This isn't about red vs. blue: it's about right vs. real. It's about rescuing a nation from the grip of spectacle, vanity, and elite delusion. If America is to endure, we need leaders who trade applause for accountability, who speak plainly, act boldly, and never forget that public office is a duty, not a spotlight.

So, take it from someone who's served, built, and led in this country: I still believe in Justice, Liberty, and Freedom for all. But not the kind peddled by the ultra-wealthy or repackaged by celebrities who mistake their fame for wisdom.

Until then, the show goes on, and the people keep losing.

And when the curtain finally falls, history won't remember the tweets, the red carpets, or the soundbites.

It will remember that a great nation crumbled, not from invasion, but from imitation.

If America falls, it would have performed its own downfall, while the world watched from the front row, laughing and live-streaming it in 4K…laughing, not out of joy, but disbelief that a superpower could collapse with such theatrical flair.

Yet, beneath that fleeting spectacle lies a profound truth. Consider this undeniable reality: for over eight decades, the United States has been the silent architect of global peace and prosperity, generously securing the stability of nations across the planet with no demand for repayment. To forget this is perilous. If America were to fall, the world as we know it would crumble, leaving a chasm of leadership that no other nation is equipped to bridge.

References

Abramowitz, A. I. (2018). The great alignment: Race, party transformation, and the rise of Donald Trump. Yale University Press. https://yalebooks.yale.edu/book/9780300245738/the-great-alignment/

AFL-CIO. (2023). Union membership statistics: 1980–2020 trends. Retrieved from https://www.aflcio.org

Annenberg Public Policy Center. (2022). Civic knowledge survey: Only 47% of Americans can name three branches of government. https://www.annenbergpublicpolicycenter.org

Associated Press. (2024, October 3). In Mesa and beyond, voters say pocketbook issues are being ignored. https://apnews.com/article/b7ccfbbbf90849834316e8c9dd164c03

Barrett, M. (2013, June 19). Arlington's $1 million bus stop draws fire. WJLA. https://wjla.com/news/local/arlington-s-1-million-bus-stop-draws-fire-87639

Braver Angels. (2024). Rebuilding civic trust across the political divide. Retrieved from https://braverangels.org

Brennan Center for Justice. (2023). Dark money basics: How secret spending affects our democracy. https://www.brennancenter.org/our-work/research-reports/dark-money-basics

Brookings. (2024, March 1). Why rural voters feel abandoned by Democrats—and how the party can win them back. https://www.brookings.edu/articles/why-rural-voters-feel-abandoned-by-democrats/

Brownstein, R. (2024, August 22). Why the Blue Wall Looms So Large. The Atlantic. https://www.theatlantic.com/politics/archive/2024/08/blue-wall-democrats-kamala-harris/679548/

Campaign Legal Center. (2024). Public financing options for federal elections. https://campaignlegal.org

Caputo, M. (2024, November 6). Democrats pile up election post-mortems. Politico. https://www.politico.com/story/2017/02/democrats-election-post-mortems-hillary-clinton-235386

Center for Humane Technology. (2023). The problem with engagement-based ranking. https://www.humanetech.com/problem

Center for Responsive Politics. (2023). OpenSecrets: Tracking money in politics. https://www.opensecrets.org

Cinelli, M., Morales, G. D. F., Galeazzi, A., Quattrociocchi, W., & Starnini, M. (2023). The echo chamber effect on social media. Proceedings of the National Academy of Sciences, 120(5), e2023301119. https://www.ncbi.nlm.nih.gov/pmc/articles/PMC7936330

CNN. (2024, October 23). Takeaways from Kamala Harris' CNN town hall. https://www.cnn.com/2024/10/23/politics/kamala-harris-town-hall-takeaways/index.html

Cohn, N. (2024, March 13). Trump gains strength in the Midwest, especially among working-class voters. The New York Times. https://www.nytimes.com/2024/03/13/us/politics/trump-midwest-working-class.html

Cramer, K. J. (2016). The politics of resentment: Rural consciousness in Wisconsin and the rise of Scott Walker. University of Chicago Press. https://press.uchicago.edu/ucp/books/book/chicago/P/bo22253304.html

Donovan, T., Tolbert, C. J., & Gracey, K. (2019). Self-reported understanding of ranked-choice voting. Social Science Quarterly, 100(5), 1768-1776.

Fair Elections Center. (2023, December). The power and limitations of celebrity political endorsements. Fair Elections Center. https://fairelectionscenter.org/media/celebrityendorsements

FairVote. (2023). Ranked Choice Voting: How it Works. Retrieved from https://www.fairvote.org/how_rcv_works

Federal Election Commission. (2023). Campaign finance data and disclosure. https://www.fec.gov

Fiorina, M. P., Abrams, S. J., & Pope, J. C. (2011). Culture war? The myth of a polarized America (3rd ed.). Pearson Longman. https://www.pearson.com/en-us/subject-catalog/p/culture-war-the-myth-of-a-polarized-america/P200000007093/9780205824280

Frum, D. (2024, July 2). Apocalypse not. The Atlantic. https://www.theatlantic.com/politics/archive/2024/07/joe-biden-democrats-convention/678863/

Frum, D. (2024, July 3). Biden's delegates are flirting with a breakup. The Atlantic. https://www.theatlantic.com/politics/archive/2024/07/democratic-delegates-joe-biden-convention/678883/

Gallup. (2023). Inflation remains top voter concern in 2023 polls. Retrieved from https://www.gallup.com

Gallup. (2024, October 5). Economy most important issue to 2024 presidential vote. Gallup.

Gallup. (2024). Majority in U.S. Still Say a Third Political Party Is Needed. Retrieved from https://news.gallup.com/poll/165392/majority-say-third-party-needed.aspx

Garthwaite, C., & Moore, T. (2013). Obama's Oprah effect: How celebrity endorsements influence political outcomes. Economics and Politics, 25(2), 217–234. https://doi.org/10.1111/ecpo.12012

Han, H. (2014). How organizations develop activists: Civic associations and leadership in the 21st century. Oxford University Press.

Harlem View. (2024, November). Celebrity endorsements: Influence on young voters in the 2024 election. https://harlemview.com/city-college/for-students/2024/11/celebrity-endorsements-influence-on-young-voters-in-the-2024-election/

Hilton, S. (2024). The new machine: How party elites reshaped the 2024 Democratic nomination. Liberty Press.

Hobbs, R. (2021). Media literacy in a digital age: Teaching the skills of critical consumption. Harvard Education Press.

Hunter, J. D. (1991). Culture Wars: The Struggle to Define America. Basic Books.

Henderson, T. (2021). The rise of celebrity politics: How pop culture reshapes elections. American Political Science Review, 115(4), 789–803. https://doi.org/10.1017/S0003055421000890

Henderson, T. (2024). The new GOP: A study of Republican adaptation and strategy in the post-Trump era. American Political Science Review, 118(1), 34–56. https://doi.org/10.1017/S000305542400034X

Hilton, A. (2021). True Blues: The Contentious Transformation of the Democratic Party. University of Pennsylvania Press. https://www.amazon.com/True-Blues-Contentious-Transformation-Democratic/dp/0812252993

Jackson, D. J. (2018). The effects of celebrity endorsements of ideas and presidential candidates. Journal of Political Marketing, 17(4), 301–322. https://doi.org/10.1080/15377857.2018.1478669

Jacobin. (2024, November 1). Kamala Harris's campaign avoided economic populism. It backfired. https://jacobin.com/2024/11/harris-campaign-economic-populism-democracy

Jones, M. (2024). The aesthetics of politics: How Instagram reshaped the 2024 campaign. Journal of Political Communication, 22(1), 78-96.

Jones, L., & Franklin, T. (2024). Understanding the swing voter: Insights from the 2024 presidential race. Oxford University Press.

Kessler, G. (2024, June 28). Fact-checking the first Biden-Trump 2024 presidential debate. The Washington Post. https://www.washingtonpost.com/politics/2024/06/28/fact-check-presidential-debate

Kirk, N. (2025). EP Thompson's moral economy and legacy. This article offers a critical commentary on historian E.P. Thompson's research into the notion of moral economy, addressing its features, methodology, and impact on subsequent scholars.

Kraus, M. W., & Tan, J. J. X. (2015). Americans overestimate social class mobility. Journal of Experimental Social Psychology, 58, 101–111. https://doi.org/10.1016/j.jesp.2014.12.007

Larsson, A. O. (2021). The rise of Instagram as a tool for political communication: A longitudinal study of European political parties and their followers. New Media & Society, 25(10), 2744–2762. https://doi.org/10.1177/14614448211034158

López, R. (2024). Beyond Likes: The Role of Influencers in Promoting Views about Feminism and Anti-Feminism in Spain. Politics & Gender, 20(3), 345-367.

https://www.cambridge.org/core/journals/politics-and-gender/article/beyond-likes-the-role-of-influencers-in-promoting-views-about-feminism-and-antifeminism-in-spain/E6A3052ED4F0B68F248C251A896BE837

McDonald, J. (2020). Media bias and the shaping of modern elections: A critical analysis. University of Chicago Press. Located in University of Chicago Press. (2020). Spring Books Catalog. University of Chicago Press. https://press.uchicago.edu/dam/ucp/books/pdf/seasonal-catalogs/spring2020_UChicagoPress_opt.pdf

Media Research Center. (2024, November 5). It's Official: 2024 Campaign News Coverage Was the Worst Ever!. MRC. https://www.newsbusters.org/blogs/nb/rich-noyes/2024/11/05/its-official-2024-campaign-news-coverage-was-worst-ever

Miller, J., & Franklin, S. (2024). The election post-mortem: Where Democrats went wrong. Politico. Retrieved from https://www.politico.com

National Center for Education Statistics. (2022). The nation's report card: Civics 2022. https://www.nationsreportcard.gov

National Review. (2024, October 25). No matter who wins, we're fiscally doomed. National Review. https://www.nationalreview.com/the-weekend-jolt/no-matter-who-wins-were-fiscally-doomed/?utm_source=chatgpt.com

Neubarth, W. (2024, November 5). Road Work Ahead: The Rust Belt Revolution is (Almost) Here! Berkeley Political Review. https://bpr.studentorg.berkeley.edu/2024/11/05/road-work-ahead-the-rust-belt-revolution-is-almost-here/

Noonan, P. (2024, February 29). We'll miss Mitch McConnell. The Wall Street Journal. https://www.wsj.com/articles/well-miss-mitch-mcconnell-american-politics-2024-campaign-trump-biden-round-two-28a209e9?utm_source=chatgpt.com

Otterbein, H., & Schneider, E. (2024, November 12). The biggest clue about the Democrats' post-election future. Politico. https://www.politico.com/news/2024/11/12/democrats-race-dnc-chair-00189112

Patterson, T. E. (2013). Informing the news: The need for knowledge-based journalism. Vintage. https://www.penguinrandomhouse.com/books/228197/informing-the-news-by-thomas-e-patterson/

Patterson, T. E. (2024, September 3). Election Beat 2024: Where are the issues? The Journalist's Resource. https://journalistsresource.org/politics-and-government/election-beat-2024-where-are-the-issues/

Pew Research Center. (2022). Public Trust in Government: 1958-2022. Retrieved from https://www.pewresearch.org

Pew Research Center. (2023). Public priorities: The gap between voters and party platforms. Retrieved from https://www.pewresearch.org

Pew Research Center. (2024). Social media engagement vs. voter turnout: Trends in the 2024 election. Retrieved from https://www.pewresearch.org

Pew Research Center. (2024). Exit polls: Economic concerns dominate 2024 election. Pew Research Center.

Pew Research Center. (2024). Voter priorities and Democratic missteps: Exit polls from the 2024 election. Pew Research Center.

Pew Research Center. (2024). Voter sentiment and economic concerns in the 2024 election.

Pew Research Center. (2024, April 9). The partisan coalitions in 2024: Trends in party identification among demographic groups. Pew

Research Center. https://www.pewresearch.org/wp-content/uploads/sites/20/2024/04/PP_2024.4.9_partisan-coalitions_REPORT.pdf

PolitiFact. (2024, April 10). Are most members of Congress millionaires?. https://www.politifact.com/factchecks/2024/apr/10/claim/are-most-members-of-congress-millionaires/

Primerica. (2023, February). National survey: Purchasing power of middle-income Americans. Primerica. https://investors.primerica.com/news-events/press-releases/detail/340/national-survey-purchasing-power-of-middle-income

Reuters. (2024, November 6). Kamala Harris made a historic dash for the White House. Here's why she fell short. https://www.reuters.com/investigations/kamala-harris-made-historic-dash-white-house-heres-why-she-fell-short-2024-11-06

Schulte, B. (2014, October 9). Desert airport sees little traffic but millions in taxpayer dollars. Center for Public Integrity. https://publicintegrity.org/national-security/desert-airport-sees-little-traffic-but-millions-in-taxpayer-dollars/

Scherer, M. (2024, November 10). Democrats wrestle with messaging failures after 2024 loss. The Washington Post. https://www.washingtonpost.com/politics/2024/11/10/democrats-2024-election-messaging

Smith, K. (2024). Lessons from the 2024 election: What Democrats need to learn. The Washington Post. Retrieved from https://www.washingtonpost.com

Street, J. (2019). Celebrity politicians: Popular culture and political representation. Polity Press. https://journals.sagepub.com/doi/10.1111/j.1467-856X.2004.00149.x

Taxpayers for Common Sense. (2012, March). 2012 Congressional Pig Book Summary. Citizens Against Government Waste. https://www.cagw.org/reporting/pig-book

Tanenhaus, S. (2025, April 2). 'Fight' recounts the 2024 election but misses its stakes. The Washington Post. https://www.washingtonpost.com/books/2025/04/02/fight-jonathan-allen-amie-parnes-trump-biden-harris-review/

Teen Vogue. (2024, September 20). The 2024 election is intertwined with music, politics and impact. https://www.teenvogue.com/story/2024-election-intertwined-music-politics-impact

The Daily Wire. (2024, November 4). Election Live-Blog: Trump Takes Back The White House. The Daily Wire. https://www.dailywire.com/news/election-live-blog-trump-kamala-hit-campaign-trail-for-last-time-in-fight-for-white-house

The Guardian. (2023, April 1). Democrats still misunderstand working-class voters—to their peril. The Guardian. https://www.theguardian.com/commentisfree/2025/apr/01/democrats-working-class-voters

The New Yorker. (2024, February 15). Bernie Sanders and Alexandria Ocasio-Cortez fight the oligarchy. https://www.newyorker.com/news/the-lede/bernie-sanders-and-alexandria-ocasio-cortez-fight-the-oligarchy

Tufekci, Z. (2023). Twitter and the architecture of amplified anger. The Atlantic. https://www.theatlantic.com/technology/archive/2023/02/twitter-anger-algorithm/672957/

U.S. Bureau of Labor Statistics. (2024). Consumer Price Index summary, 2020-2024. Retrieved from https://www.bls.gov

U.S. Department of the Treasury. (2025, April 4). The debt to the penny. Bureau of the Fiscal Service. https://fiscaldata.treasury.gov/datasets/debt-to-the-penny/debt-to-the-penny

Vincent, J. (2024, November 14). Pro-Harris TikTok felt safe in an algorithmic bubble—until Election Day. The Verge. https://www.theverge.com/2024/11/14/24295814/kamala-harris-tiktok-filter-bubble-donald-trump-algorithm https://www.theverge.com/2024/11/14/24295814/kamala-harris-tiktok-filter-bubble-donald-trump-algorithm

Wood, Natalie & Herbst, Kenneth. (2007). Political Star Power and Political Parties. Journal of Political Marketing. 6. 141-158. 10.1300/J199v06n02_08.

About the Author

Dr. Douglas B. Sims is a highly respected environmental soil scientist with over 30 years of experience in the environmental consulting industry. He holds a bachelor's and a master's degree from the University of Nevada, Las Vegas, and a Ph.D. from Kingston University London, establishing a strong foundation in environmental science and scholarly research.

In 2011, Dr. Sims transitioned from the private sector to academia, joining the College of Southern Nevada (CSN) as an environmental science instructor. His deep expertise and visionary leadership led to his appointment as Dean of the School of Science, Engineering, and Mathematics at CSN. In this role, he has been instrumental in aligning academic programs with industry needs, preparing students for successful careers in science and engineering.

Throughout his career, Dr. Sims has remained an active researcher, publishing extensively in peer-reviewed journals on subjects such as soil and water contamination. His work has had a lasting impact, contributing meaningfully to both academic discourse and real-world environmental practices.

In addition to his scientific and academic accomplishments, Dr. Sims is deeply committed to education and student success. He has played a vital role in developing innovative programs that support workforce readiness and has mentored countless students pursuing careers in environmental science.

Beyond his professional life, Dr. Sims is an avid observer of human behavior, particularly intrigued by the intersection of American politics and social issues. His ability to connect scientific thinking with broader societal challenges allows him to offer unique insights across disciplines.

Married to his college sweetheart since the mid-1990s, He and his wife have raised two kids and remain deeply committed to family, education, and lifelong curiosity about the world.

www.ingramcontent.com/pod-product-compliance
Lightning Source LLC
Chambersburg PA
CBHW060226030426
42335CB00014B/1345